OUT WITH THE STARS

HOLLYWOOD NIGHTLIFE IN THE GOLDEN ERA

JIM HEIMANN

ABBEVILLE PRESS · PUBLISHERS · NEW YORK

This book is dedicated to two North American Aviation riveters whose swingshift exploits at the Palladium, the Zamboanga, Patmar's, the Rollerdrome, Okie Palladium, and the Aragon Ballroom served as my inspiration—Mom and Dad.

Editor: Walton Rawls
Designer: 90 Degrees / Valerie Sutphin
Copyeditor: Don Goddard
Production Manager: Dana Cole
Production Editor: Robin James

Library of Congress Cataloging in Publication Data
Heimann, Jim.
  Out with the stars.

  Includes index.
  1. Restaurants, lunch rooms, etc.—California—
Hollywood. 2. Music-halls (Variety-theaters,
cabarets, etc.—California—Hollywood (Calif.)—
Social life and customs. I. Title.
TX909.H36 1985   979.4'94   85-15719
ISBN 0-89659-572-2

ACKNOWLEDGMENTS

In the decade since I first began digging into Hollywood's nightclub past, a vast number of individuals assisted me in my research and in the eventual publication of this book. Among those who deserve special thanks and attention are the following: David Boule, Chris DeNoon, and Freda Wheatley-Vizcarra for their sheer dedication to this project in researching, typing, and cheering me on; Catherine Boyer for her very professional (and discounted) editing services; Valerie Sutphin and Henry Vizcarra for their more than generous time in designing the book; Paul Mussa for his design input; Ed Whittington (whose unselfishness and concern for history overshadowed material gain) and his three-generation family of photographers who have preserved a detailed and magical time-machine look at the Southern California landscape; the Kobal Collection for the cover photograph; Lee Pisarski for his retouching; Bob Rodriguez for his talents; all those who relived this era through their oral histories, including Tony Martin, Andy Albracht, Rose and Ronnie Young, and the Quintana family; those who provided photos and memorabilia, including Joe Jasgur, Bison Archives, Bruce Henstell, Bruce Torrence, Tom Zimmerman, and Dave Marshall; Walton Rawls for his patience and guidance in the entire book-production process and his prowess as an editor; and to all the institutions and libraries who gave of their time and facilities in the quest for historical accuracy. For those I have inadvertently not mentioned specifically, my sincere apologies.

Every effort has been made to secure permission and provide appropriate credit for photographic material and text in publications no longer active; the author deeply regrets any omissions and pledges to correct errors called to his attention in subsequent editions.

CONTENTS

Sebastian
CAFE
Sebastian
CAFE
VENICE
PLUNGE
VENICE
PLUNGE
VENICE
PLUNGE

EARLY HOLLYWOOD

When the first motion picture company set up shop in Southern California in 1909, Los Angeles and its environs could offer few diversions to newly arrived Easterners. Chute's Amusement Park at Main and Washington streets, Crawston's Pasadena Ostrich Farm, rowboats on Eastlake Park's large pond, and the Alligator Farm in East L.A. were a far cry from the more sophisticated delights of cosmopolitan Gotham. Those interested in the sporting life found the climate accommodating for horseracing at Ascot Park in the hinterlands of South Central Los Angeles, football games and chariot races at Pasadena's annual Tournament of Roses, and the pugilistic encounters offered by heavyweight champ Jim Jeffries in the blue smoke-drenched ambiance of the Vernon Arena. Tourists were drawn by the wealth and beauty of the land, which the Los Angeles Chamber of Commerce promoted to the hilt, but what happened after sunset was of little concern. Oranges, beaches, and climate made the money—not music, booze and mayhem. Though the area was not exactly sleepy, its outlets for casual carousing, especially at night, were thin indeed.

As the suburb of Hollywood began to accumulate motion picture studios, it also attracted a steady stream of actors and actresses and related film personnel from the East. In this conservative town of bean and poppy fields, the small film community was soon ostracized by the old-timers, who found their filming in the streets and sometimes loose habits too much to handle. The Hollywood Hotel, which opened in 1903 for the benefit of tourists flocking to see the surrounding natural wonders and painter Paul de Longpre's famed gardens, became the obvious focus for social functions. Located on Hollywood Boulevard at Highland, its imposing size and Mission–Moorish styling made it a landmark and a mecca for actors when they first hit town. Not knowing how long they might be employed in California, many of the transplanted actors set up housekeeping there before settling into the surrounding area on a permanent basis. In town, one was more likely to see a stray coyote ramble down the street than an establishment like New York's Delmonico's. It was the country. A famous quote of the period suggests its underdevelopment: "After nine o'clock, you could shoot a cannon down Hollywood Boulevard, and never hit anybody." Eventually, Thursday night became the social time, when the lobby of the Hollywood Hotel would be cleared and dancing allowed by the proprietress, Mira Hershey (of chocolate fame). Mrs. Hershey was also the unofficial chaperone, who made sure no one drank or indulged in other forbidden sweets while she was on duty.

The Hollywood Hotel was a phenomenal success, and the legions of stars who passed through it in subsequent decades loaded the registry with so many famous autographs that the book was eventually given to the Smithsonian for posterity.

For those in the movie colony who

A bevy of beauties parades in front of Frank Sebastian's Windward Avenue cafe in Venice.

Above. The Hollywood Hotel, in the heart of town, was the first spot in Hollywood proper for nightlife.

Opposite. The Alexandria Hotel at Spring and Eighth streets in downtown Los Angeles played host to the film colony's early stars.

tired of the Thursday night soirées on Hollywood Boulevard, a short trip to downtown Los Angeles opened up more sophisticated entertainment. Central L.A. was still the financial and business center of the city and, consequently, the social center also. Since quite a few studios were still located near the downtown district, along with theaters and motion picture houses, established hotels such as the Van Nuys and the Alexandria catered in a much more real way to the professional and social needs of the fledgling film community. Here, night life was a bit more brisk, and a variety of decent meals could be found in the district. The Alexandria, in particular, was a meeting ground for producers, directors, and actors. At Fifth and Spring since 1906, the hotel had hosted royalty, as well as presidents, and it was a natural gathering spot for the rising aristocracy of the "movies." The lobby, ornately appointed with crystal chandeliers, marble columns, potted palms, and a thick rug called the "million dollar carpet" (because of the deals that transpired on it), was the afternoon meeting place. The bar, offering cocktails and free sandwiches, enjoyed lively conversation, and many an out-of-work actor found himself there for contacts, as well as the free bites. It was here, in 1918, that Rudolph Valentino, new in town, sought the camaraderie of his fellow actors, eventually picking up a few leads that gave him his break in the movies. Jack Warner lived at the Alexandria for several years. Herbert Somborn (who

would establish the Brown Derby restaurant), was introduced to Gloria Swanson in the Alexandria dining room, and, soon afterward, they were married.

On neighboring streets, the deals and socializing spilled over to local hangouts such as Al Levy's place at Third and Main, which displayed atop its roof the pushcart from which Al vended oysters in front of theaters before he achieved success. At Sixth and Hope was Ye Bull Pen, attracting some of the sporting crowd. Back on Spring Street, the largest collection of pre-1920s bars, dance halls, and cafes blazed seductive lights to the incubating movie crowd. It seemed every other shop housed an open-air cigar counter, where rolling dice and lottery tickets were freely dispensed. The Imperial Cafe boasted of being the longest—it ran the block between Spring and Broadway, above which was a balcony preferred by women and their escorts. The Hoffman Bar was known as the hangout for studio technicians, and nearby, between Fourth and Sixth streets, the Rathskeller was the poor man's Alexandria. McKee's Restaurant included a floor show, while nearby Harlow's competed for customers by offering Los Angeles's first ice ballet on a skating rink installed on its stage. Barney Oldfield, race-car driver supreme, operated the Western Athletic Club, sponsoring prizefights on Saturday nights. With its endless procession of nighteries, Spring Street was beginning to advertise itself as the Great White Way West. The entertainment venues downtown clearly had

9

10

The Vernon Country Club, Hollywood's first bona fide nightclub, was situated, in true roadhouse fashion, in the midst of beet fields.

an advantage over the pastoral pastimes in Hollywood, and although the movie studios increasingly gravitated to Hollywood, the film colony preferred its merrymaking outside the workplace, venturing to the wild and woolly hinterlands even beyond Los Angeles's jurisdiction.

Within the city of Los Angeles, the overwhelmingly reformist and Protestant populace had either outlawed or substantially watered down the city's vices. The Women's Christian Temperance Union was on the move toward prohibition, and ordinances either banned or limited the places where dancing and booze could mix. But for those municipalities unhampered by blue laws, the Los Angeles outskirts could offer a variety of nocturnal attractions.

Enter Baron Long, who with his triad of clubs in Vernon, Watts, and Venice ushered in the true nightclub era of Hollywood. Born in Indiana, the Baron, as he was known, ventured into Los Angeles by way of a stint in San Francisco selling patent medicine. In Los Angeles, he became assistant to Jim Jeffries, who promoted boxing matches in the Vernon Arena at Thirty-Ninth Street and Santa Fe. Vernon was one of those independent towns known throughout Southern California as a place where things were pretty much out in the open and not subject to L.A.'s legal bindings. Vernon's reputation as a boxing capital was supplemented by sports promoter Jack Doyle's famous watering hole, and together they spelled out Vernon as *the* place to be for

a good time. The Baron knew the grass was greener in this neck of the woods, and he jumped into the bar trade on May 2, 1912, when he opened the Vernon Country Club at Forty-Ninth and Santa Fe. From the day the doors opened until the place burned down in March 1929, it was a complete success.

The bar's appearance was hardly glamorous compared to later clubs. It was a roadhouse, pure and simple, set in the middle of beet fields, and there was a broad parking lot between it and the street. But it became the birthplace for Hollywood nightlife, and the spawning ground for countless entertainers and restaurant men. The entertainment at first consisted of a violin, piano, and trap drummer. Directed by Max Fisher, the band was later supplemented by saxophonist Rudolph Weidoff and Paul Whiteman on violin. It was said that the Vernon introduced jazz to Southern California, and that, teamed up with a liberal drinking policy, soon had the Hollywood crowd making the drive out to the club. Night after night, Fatty Arbuckle, Mary Pickford, Gloria Swanson, Wallace Reid, D. W. Griffith, and the cream of early Hollywood personalities streamed in. Private parties abounded. At one, Fatty Arbuckle grabbed a steak, slapped it between two pieces of bread, and then consumed the massive sandwich. "Steak Sandwich" appeared on the menu soon afterward, and a culinary tradition was born. Tom Mix drove his car into the club, and once inside, announced who he was

11

Opposite. Built in 1905 on the Venice pier, the Ship Cafe was a popular rendezvous of movie stars for several decades.

Part of early club-owner Baron Long's triumvirate, the Ship Cafe offered a bountiful feast from this circa 1917 menu.

and bought everyone in the place a drink. Sophie Tucker dressed up as Santa Claus for several years and refused to give·up the position. The club was a favorite for location filming, and Anna May Wong made her motion picture debut there. Rudolph Valentino, before he hit the big time, was employed as a tango dancer for thirty-five dollars a week. The Baron claimed he fired him. Valentino's version was that there were greener pastures in Pasadena that offered him more money to tango. Gambling was conducted in the smoky recesses, and vice cases against Long were mysteriously dismissed. Even during Prohibition, no one went thirsty. Long's uncanny ability as talent scout secured the services of Abe Lyman, Harry Richman, Gus Arnheim, and Mrs. Vernon Castle long before they had made it big. The integration of floor show, dancing, chorus girls, and orchestra—another Baron Long innovation—became standard for nightclubs in years to come. Even employees got a fair shake from the Baron, who seldom fired anybody but levied fines for regulation infringements and put the money into a pool he would match at year's end. The fund grew large enough for employees to borrow from it, interest-free, to build homes, launch businesses, and cover emergencies. Needless to say, workers stuck around.

Across town was another of Long's success stories, the Ship Cafe, built in 1905 on a pier in Albert Kinney's fantasy-by-the-sea: Venice. Originally run by Carlo Marchetti, who later opened a down-

The interior of the Ship Cafe in its fashionable heyday.

town eatery, the combination hotel-restaurant was a natural magnet for movie stars. Named the "Cabrillo," it was fashioned after a Spanish galleon and served up high-priced cuisine in the main dining room, or in private salons on the second deck. The staff were uniformed like sixteenth-century naval officers, and, as in most places outside Los Angeles, hootch was available to any well-heeled customer who could afford it. The Ship was available for private functions, which many of Hollywood's rising stars preferred, and the mayhem that attended New Year's Eve made for headline copy. It was at the Ship that Valentino had his heels cooled by movie queen Nazimova, who called him a "pimp" and a "gigolo" at a private party she was throwing for co-workers at Metro. And it was Buster Keaton who, pestered by autograph hounds, jumped out of one of the restaurant's portholes in a faked escape attempt, only to find twice as many fans when he returned.

The Ship continued its boisterous activities despite a fire and reconstruction in 1924, several name changes (it was briefly the Showboat Cafe), and management shifts (from Baron Long to the Lyman Brothers and on to Tommy Jacobs, who remodeled it in 1933 for $50,000). But its heyday was before the Depression, and it slipped into obscurity, eventually to be razed in October 1946.

The beach cities, with their enormous appeal, extended beyond Venice-By-The-Sea. Fraser's Million-Dollar Pier in Ocean Park was a maze of noodle houses, lunch-

The Ship
Dancing Contest
TO-NIGHT
New Year's Eve
Dinner De Luxe
Reservations $5 per Cover
VENICE-BY-THE-SEA

15

rooms, opium dens, roller coasters, theaters, and ballyhoo. A few blocks north, at the end of Hollister Avenue, was Nat Goodwin's Pier and Cafe—a spot that rivaled the Ship in star attendance. A crystal confection by night, it was buoyed by strings of electric lights, and billed itself as a high-class cabaret where there was never a dull moment. The pier had a sun parlor, a roof garden, a ballroom, and parking accommodations for 350 automobiles. "Marrying Nat" (eight marriages earned Goodwin the nickname) was considered one of the great light comedians of the stage by many, including Charlie Chaplin, who in 1916 lived in Santa Monica and frequented the Cafe. Chaplin often took long walks along the beach with Goodwin after dining. According to her biography, Mabel Normand, the freewheeling ingenue of her day, attempted suicide off Goodwin's Pier in 1915 after finding sweetheart Mack Sennett in a compromising situation with a mutual movie pal.

Dancing to jazz bands was forbidden in Hollywood but not along the coast. Ballrooms such as the Egyptian, the Bon Ton, the Venice, and the Three O'Clock held enormous crowds. They sponsored "movie nights," where studios paraded their local protégés. Even without the limelight, movie folk could slip unnoticed into Schleuter's Dance Palace and give a try at the Chicken Shuffle, the "newest and greatest dance comedy of 1916."

In Santa Monica, below the bluffs, was

16

Above. Nat Goodwin's Cafe was built on a private pier at the foot of Hollister Avenue in Ocean Park.

Opposite above. The entrance to Nat Goodwin's first-class cabaret, which boasted a sun parlor, roof garden, and ballroom.

Opposite below. The interior of Nat Goodwin's Cafe, frequented by such notables as Charlie Chaplin, Mabel Normand, and Mack Sennett.

Left. The Three O'clock Ballroom in Venice offered the forbidden delight of public dancing, which was outlawed back in Hollywood.

Below. Danceland, in the wild and wooly suburb of Culver City, was an enormous open-air dance emporium with space to park 3,500 autos. Later it would be the site of the Circus Maximus in MGM's 1925 epic Ben Hur.

Opposite. With jazz band on hand, merrymakers at the Cinderella Roof Ballroom prepare to enter a new decade.

18

20

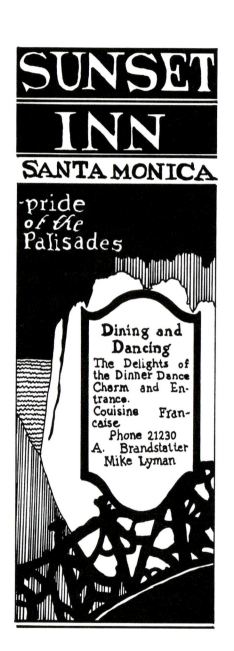

The Sunset Inn, below the bluffs of Santa Monica, was the zenith of pre-Prohibition Hollywood nightlife.

the Sunset Inn, the Pride of the Palisades, which, when it was run by Baron Long, eclipsed the Ship Cafe and the Vernon Country Club in popularity. Abe Lyman played there for dancing contests and carnival nights at which Wallace Reid, Charlie Chaplin, Fatty Arbuckle, Buster Keaton, and the rest of the silent gang would stay until closing. Cinema flapper Coleen Moore remembered Bebe Daniels and Harold Lloyd being the best dancers and getting shelves of trophies for their efforts. When Mike Lyman and Eddie Brandstatter took over the Inn, Thursday nights became the evening to spot a boatload of film folk. A five-dollar cover charge kept the riff-raff out, but once inside, the entertainment and jokes by screenland greats were well worth the price. The owners singled out a star to honor weekly, calling the nights ''Fillum Fotoplayer Food Festivals,'' and gave sobriquets like ''Mammoth Olives a la Roscoe Arbuckle,'' ''Shrimp Cocktail a la Buster Keaton,'' and ''Chicken a la Fanny Ward'' to special dishes for the night.

As the postwar era came to a close, the innocence of Hollywood's early days, held so dearly in the memory of its pioneers, faded into the businesslike atmosphere of corporate moviemaking. As massive profits, salaries, and star build-ups became dominant issues, the industry embarked on the roller-coaster ride of its teen years with a whole new set of standards for making whoopee after dark.

21

THE TWENTIES

On June 30, 1919, Prohibition, which had hung over the nation's head for the better part of ten years, finally became law. Gone were the days when liquor ran free, and in came a brand new way of seeking nighttime sport. Speakeasies, rumrunning, gambling, and guns slid the whole country into one delirious decade.

But before John Barleycorn was laid to rest, L.A.'s nightspots had one final fling that Sunday night. In Vernon, as many as 50,000 patrons formed swirling masses in the streets, going nowhere. Jack Doyle's and the Vernon Country Club flowed with booze, and throngs guzzled everything in sight, making New Year's celebrations look like child's play. Hundreds of automobiles clogged the streets, closing them off in one huge traffic jam that would last until six o'clock the following morning. At the Vernon Country Club, normally two-dollar tables were fifty dollars apiece, and by 9 P.M., all of them were occupied. The club's usual capacity of a few hundred had swollen to over 2,000. Meanwhile, in Venice, an estimated 100,000 revelers jammed the resort, closing off all available avenues into the town. Tables at the Ship Cafe went for three-hundred dollars, and doors were closed at 10 P.M. after capacity had long since been reached. A funeral procession of "girls in YamaYama suits and men in grotesque costume" snaked through the streets, playing dirges lamenting the deaths of Gambrinus and John Barleycorn. At midnight, the taps were turned off, and the orgy climaxed in an explosion of fireworks, auto horns, and whistles. California was "dry."

Jack Doyle's closed forever. The Vernon announced it would follow suit when beer was outlawed, but six months later was advising customers: "bring your own." The Ship also flourished through the 1920s, and the only loser seemed to be the law.

On Washington Boulevard in Culver City, Prohibition launched a fertile succession of dance halls, cabarets, and speakeasies that overshadowed those in Venice and Vernon during the '20s. Because the town was fast becoming the area's second Hollywood, with studios sprouting up everywhere, movie folk were in abundance. As early as 1915, Thomas Ince had established his studio on Washington Boulevard. Mergers transformed his original site into Triangle Studios, and he moved to another site, also on Washington. Eventually, Culver City became known as the "Heart of Screenland," and in the '20s, MGM, Willat, and Hal Roach all called Culver City home. Washington Boulevard, on which most of the studios faced, was one of the main corridors between downtown L.A. and the beach communities. Venice Boulevard, nearby, was serviced by the Pacific Electric's Red Car tracks, which made Culver conveniently close for all of the Southland. Culver City's autonomy, like Vernon's and Venice's, proved irresistible to purveyors of illegal fun. With Prohibition, Washington Boulevard mushroomed into a mall of nightspots in

The essence of silent-era glamour in Hollywood was a night at the world-famous Cocoanut Grove.

24

Masquerading as dining spots, roadhouses such as Moonlite Gardens and Ford's Castle proliferated along Washington Boulevard in Culver City.

the midst of farmland and movie studios.

In open land, early clubs along the strip looked like sedate farmhouses and country clubs. Moonlite Gardens and Ford's Castle, surrounded by eucalyptus and palms, hardly seemed the settings for cinema hi-jinks. But beyond the advertised chicken and frog's legs dinners, a good bottle of gin and a snappy jazz tune prevailed. Danceland, an open-air ballroom on Washington near Adams with a marble dance floor and Speed Webb and his Colored Melody Lads, graphically illustrated how sparse the landscape was by advertising free parking for three thousand cars on the lot next door. (In 1925, this tract of land would be transformed into the Circus Maximus for MGM's *Ben Hur*.)

In 1923, construction began for one of the Southland's largest entertainment emporiums. The Green Mill, at the intersection of National and Washington, was a full-blown Normandy concoction of architecture, occupying a block-wide site. Built by local contractor Dan Coombs and managed by Louis Spielman, it would begin in 1926 its reign as Frank Sebastian's Cotton Club, the ultimate Prohibition L.A. nightspot, which, after stints as the Casa Mañana and Meadowbrook Gardens, would burn to the ground in 1948.

By 1926, bootleggers, prostitutes, gamblers, and a host of unsavory characters had nestled comfortably into Culver City's rural ''Great White Way,'' and the movie set was more than obliged to

The Green Mill at Washington and National boulevards opened in 1923 and housed a long succession of dance halls until it burned down in 1948.

sample the wares at the DooDoo Inn, the Kit Kat Club, Monkey Farm, Hoosegow, Club Royale, Harlow's Cafe, Midnight Frolics, and the Sneak Inn. After-hours snacks could be had at the Chicken Roost, the Lighthouse, Tommy Ryan's Diner, Fil'm Hut Tea Room, and King's Tropical Inn. It was wall-to-wall mayhem, and the small police force did little to keep pace with the lawbreakers. Raids netted only small caches of hootch, and those sometimes turned up in the lawmen's flasks. Rumrunners swarmed along the coast, and Washington Boulevard went straight down to Playa Del Rey, a well known drop-off point for vessels such as the *Sassy Lass*. "Wide Open" was an understatement for the activities along the Boulevard.

Frank Sebastian, another of L.A.'s leading entertainment men, knew opportunity when he saw it. His successful Sebastian's Cafe on Windward Avenue, in the heart of Venice, prompted him to open an even larger place, and Washington reeked of success. Taking over the Green Mill, he transformed the massive ballroom with a mesh of styles. From its Oriental tentlike interior to the French château exterior outlined in neon, the new Cotton Club perfectly mirrored the zany jazzbo's stomping on its floors. "The King of Cabarets" was the first to exclusively feature "colored" orchestras and Creole Revues on the West Coast, and Sebastian's pioneering efforts gave cinema stars a rare chance to sample the sounds that were being heard at its name-

25

King's Tropical Inn at Washington and Adams, the Chicken Roost at 5738 Washington Boulevard, and the Hoosegow, also on Washington, were just a few of the 1920s nitespots in Culver City.

Below. King's Tropical Inn, interior.

26

sake in New York. Les Hite, Lionel Hampton, V. Elkin and His Ten Cotton Pickers, Cab Calloway, Duke Ellington, Louis Armstrong, and virtually every black act that toured made an appearance at Sebastian's. Ellington trombonist Lawrence Brown deemed the club far better than the one in Harlem. The affable Sebastian knew how to throw a jazz-age party every night, and always with class. New Years were special affairs, with three dance bands on separate floors, four different revues with a cast of forty-two, souvenirs, favors, dancing 'til dawn, and a ham-and-egg breakfast with Frank for up to 2,000 patrons who lasted the evening. Prices?—$5.00 to $7.50, inclusive. Star entertainers fared almost as well in private balcony-level dressing rooms, with sets and bandstands costing up to $200,000. In addition to the lavish setup offered at the Cotton Club, gambling was rumored to be available in the back room, and several slot machines stood in the lobby at one time. Louis Armstrong, making his first appearance on the West Coast, was arrested for possession of marijuana, along with a musician in Abe Lyman's band, between sets in the back of the club in November 1930. Describing it as a setup, Armstrong's biographer proposed that a rival club or gang interested in the performer's services arranged the arrest. "Connections" set the two free, and Sebastian's business went on as if nothing had ever happened.

The Plantation Cafe on the other end

27

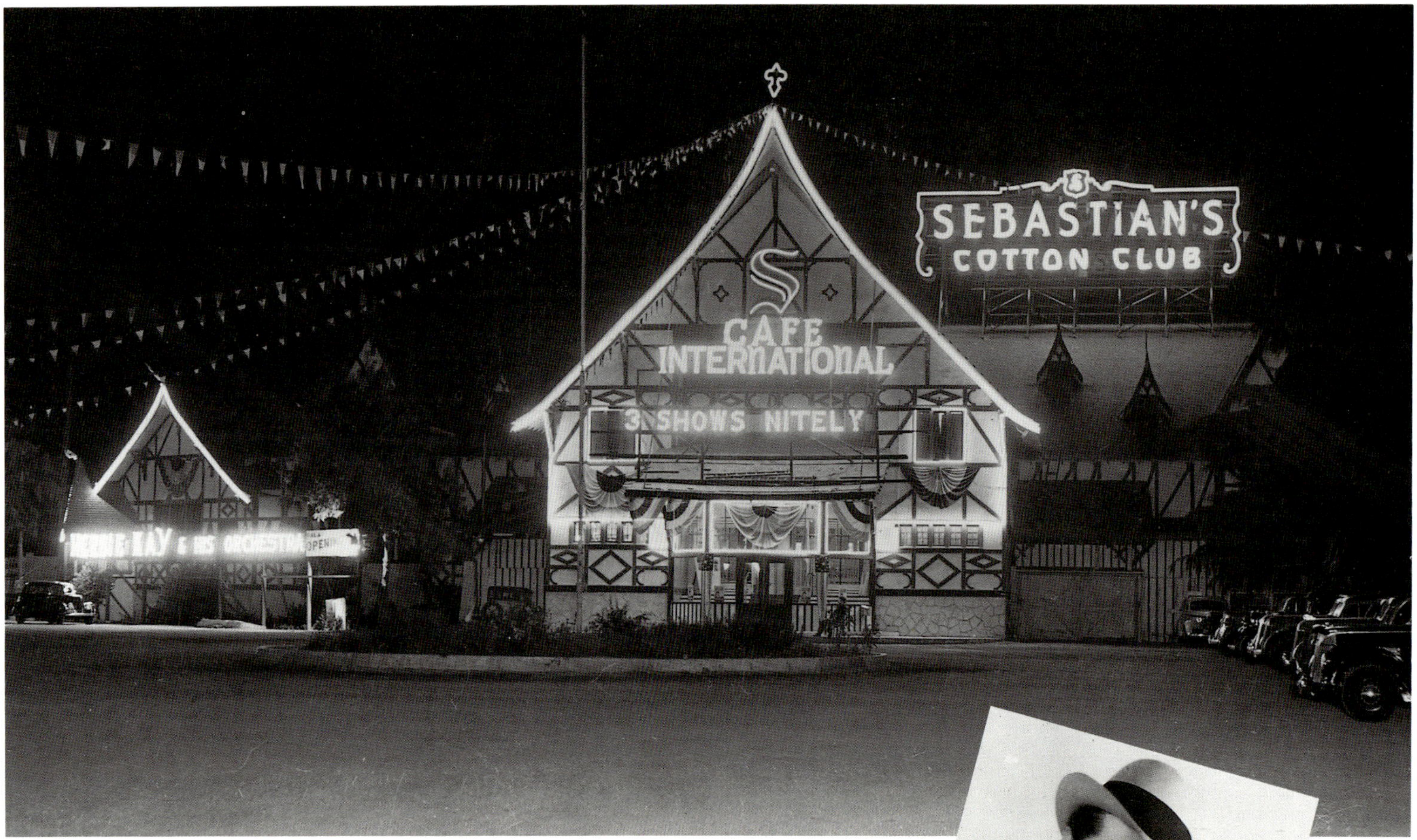
SEBASTIAN'S
COTTON CLUB
CAFE
INTERNATIONAL
3 SHOWS NITELY

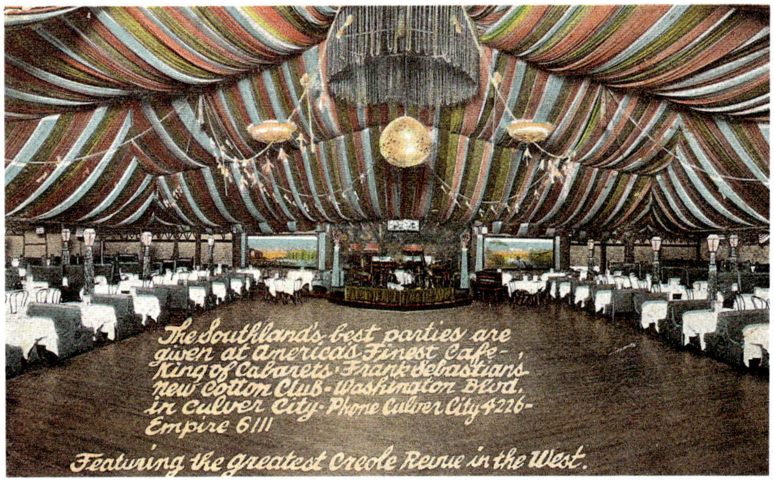
The Southland's best parties are given at America's Finest Cafe - King of Cabarets · Frank Sebastian's New Cotton Club · Washington Blvd. in Culver City · Phone Culver City 4226 - Empire 6111
Featuring the greatest Creole Revue in the West.

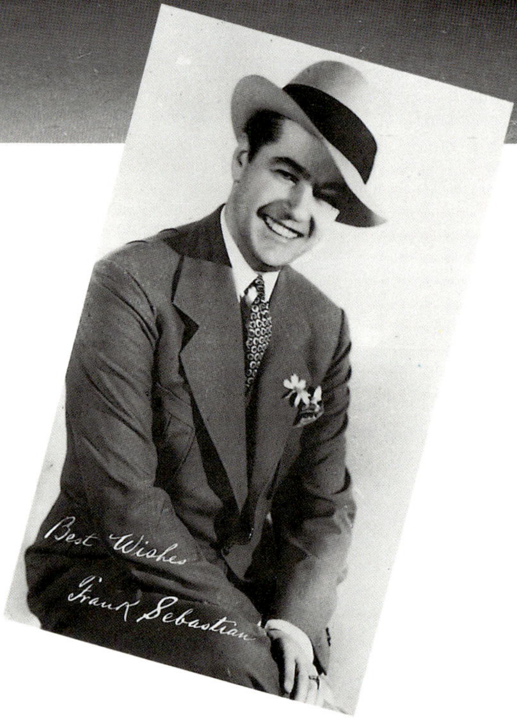
Best Wishes
Frank Sebastian

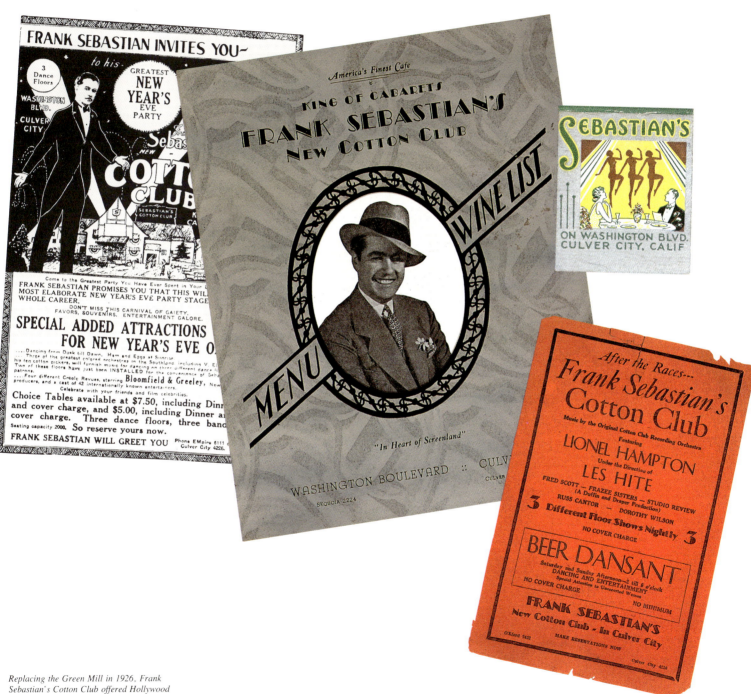

Replacing the Green Mill in 1926, Frank Sebastian's Cotton Club offered Hollywood the hottest jazz attractions.

Roscoe ''Fatty'' Arbuckle's Plantation Cafe
on Washington Boulevard's western terminus
opened in 1926.

of Washington was the Western terminus of the Boulevard's playground. Roscoe ''Fatty'' Arbuckle opened his cafe on August 2, 1928, in the former Plantation Club, on the rebound from the disastrous trial and scandal that ruined his movie career. Dan Coombs, builder of the Cotton Club, was asked to rebuild the burned-out Plantation to Fatty's specifications within twenty-eight days, and he did. A guilt-ridden Hollywood community, which had abandoned him earlier, rose to the occasion when Fatty's funds fell short and donated its services. MGM art director Cedric Gibbons did the interior decoration, which was described as great stretches of painted canvas suspended from the ceiling and strung with electric lights like stars. Opening night drew the entire film community in a show of support for the comedian's new venture. Among the guests were Charlie Chaplin, Buster Keaton, Mary Pickford, Tom Mix, Douglas Fairbanks, Harry Langdon, Bebe Daniels, Ruth Roland, Lew Cody, and Constance and Norma Talmadge. Mabel Normand gave him a life-size floral effigy of himself, Fatty performed his routine to rousing applause, and the club succeeded until the Stock Market crashed—he sold it in 1930. For its several frantic years, celebrities scurried between it and Sebastian's for the best entertainment in the area. On the menu was printed: ''Guests are requested not to embarrass the management by bringing intoxicating liquors into the establishment''—an admonishment indicating Fatty wanted no

31

Above. Plantation Club entrance on Washington Boulevard looking east toward Overland Avenue and MGM.

Plantation Club interior, in 1929.

Opposite above. The Red Nichols Band on the porch of the Plantation Club in 1928.

Opposite below. Will Morrissey and Midgie Miller pose with Plantation Club chorines in 1927.

further part in wrongdoing.

If Culver City represented the bawdy side of nightlife, events closer to Hollywood indicated a new breed of sophistication was about to bud. The money the movie industry poured into Hollywood made it apparent that the days of dusty roads and little-known feature players were at an end. As pepper trees and bean fields rapidly disappeared, hordes of movie-struck citizens bounded into Hollywood, lured by million-dollar salaries and fame beyond comprehension. Los Angeles was experiencing one of the largest population booms of its existence, and the capital being invested was spreading the city in all directions. The Ambassador Hotel was built in 1920 on a stretch of Wilshire Boulevard that was considered "out of town." Planners anticipated the city's growth westward, and Wilshire Boulevard became the main thoroughfare of the expansion. The smart set was settling in nearby land developments. To complement the downtown hostelries, the Ambassador was designed to accommodate the influx of visitors being beckoned by city boosters, whose miles of prose glorified the land of oranges, flowers, and endless sunshine. Wintering tourists were the first guests to stay at the Ambassador when it opened on New Year's Day, 1921. Perched on a hilltop, the hotel commanded unobstructed views from the Hollywood Hills to Catalina Island. The grounds were groomed with velvet lawns and tropical vegetation, and its popularity with the film community was immediate.

33

Below. The Ambassador Hotel was an immediate success with Hollywood luminaries when it opened on New Year's Day, 1921.

Opposite above. The Cocoanut Grove in 1922.

Opposite below. The Ambassador's Parrot Porch adjoined the Zinnia Room, forerunner of the Cocoanut Grove.

The four hundred rooms and bungalows were home to Wilson Mizner, John Barrymore, Pola Negri, Norma Talmadge, Scott and Zelda Fitzgerald, and whoever else landed in Hollywood and wanted deluxe lodging. The Zinnia Grill, on the Casino level of the hotel, quickly became the nighttime meeting place of hotel guests and the visiting movie crowd. With walls of black satin, hand-painted with colorful zinnias, the club was dubbed the "Black Patent Leather Room," and dancers could rest in the adjoining Parrot Porch, amidst squawking canaries, parrots, and blooming plants. The management, noting the lines of people attending the room every night, sensed the Ambassador could easily accommodate a full-scale nightclub, and plans for converting the Grand Ballroom into the Cocoanut Grove were completed on April 21, 1921. The opening-night crowd was unaware of what the decor or policy of the room would be, and the invitations carefully avoided description. First-nighters entered a grove of imitation palm trees nailed to the hardwood ballroom floor, with fake monkeys scrambling up the trunks and Chinese lanterns strung between the fronds. Simple bent-cane chairs lined the tables, and on one wall, a mural of tropical mountains and cataracts heightened the illusion of a Pacific paradise. The evening's music was provided by Art Hickman's jazz band.

In a *Photoplay* article, longtime maitre d' Jimmy Manos revealed that the Grove's decor came courtesty of several hundred prop palms left over from the

35

Opposite. The Montmartre, on the second floor of 6757 Hollywood Boulevard, in 1926.

Below. A fashionable luncheon crowd leaving the Montmartre.

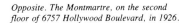

filming of Valentino's *The Sheik*. Bought cheaply, they constituted the bulk of the Grove's decor until a more lavish scheme of Moorish design was instituted. Compared to some of the earlier nightspots with their sparse trimmings, the Cocoanut Grove was pure style. The film hierarchy booked banquets in the thousand-seat Grove almost as soon as the doors opened, and opening night witnessed two stars punching it out in what was to become a Grove tradition. As in almost any other place in Los Angeles, liquor was available, though not by official policy. On nights when a big shindig was planned, long lines of limousines would drive up to the Ambassador's porte cochere and deposit heavy suitcases. Later in the evening, guests who had made provision ahead could find their beverages discreetly placed under their table. In the early years, Chaplin could be coaxed to provide impromptu entertainment, but almost from the first the management offered guests lots to do. Tuesday night was star night, and elaborate floor shows accompanied the mass arrival of stars— all competing for the most dramatic appearance at the Grove's main entrance.

When the Charleston became the dance sensation, dance contests were held for prize silver trophies. Judges were recruited from the hoipolloi of filmdom, and the dance floor at the Grove was the place to be. Joan Crawford, in her Lucille LeSeur days, was considered the hottest dancer at the Grove. She and debonair dance partner Michael Cudahy, a meat-

Fans crowd the Montmartre entrance hoping
to glimpse their favorite stars.

38

packing heir, would swoop over the floor madly competing for the coveted trophy with Carole Lombard, who was still Jean Peters then, and her partner. Joan was usually with the MGM contingent, while Carole's crowd included local kids Tommy Lee, Loretta Young, and her sisters. Joan Crawford's enthusiasm certainly was noticed, and in *Screwball*, Lombard's biography, Carole recalled: "Joan had great body tension. She was better than I, but she seemed to be working at it, and for me it was all play. It was a thrill to beat her, and she liked to beat me, too. But that wasn't the big thing with her. She didn't just want to get a start in pictures, she kept talking about reaching the top." For other winners, a movie contract wasn't that important. The trophies were redeemable with the Grove management for their fifteen-dollar cost, and many of the dancers, mostly in their teens, gladly hocked the silver prizes for the money. May McAvoy redeemed her cache for three hundred dollars.

Almost a year after the Grove opened, the first floor show was presented, featuring Maurice and Lenora Hughes, continental sensations of the skating waltz. Their engagement was followed by that of Sidar Remmi Setti, a grand mental telepathist, and then the "Great Night Frolic," a show in the Ziegfeld tradition. For these bills, the Grove continued hiring the best musical talent available. All the early white jazz musicians were booked there, including Abe Lyman, Ted Fio Rito, Gus Arnheim, and Jimmie Grier,

Leatrice Joy and Raquel Torrey sign in at the Montmartre.

The luncheon crowd at the Montmartre.

for extended engagements. They often played on Fridays, another Grove specialty night, when collegians were invited to patch up rivalries on the dance floor. Collegiate Night also gave revelers a chance to spike the Grove's dollar-and-a-half pitcher of tropical punch, and compete in the dance contests. On other nights, a more extravagant entertainment policy was in effect. Floor shows included a parade of briefly attired chorines perched atop floats that circled the dance floor. Elaborate dolls in centerpieces and toy monkeys that descended from the balcony on strings had stars with six-figure incomes scrambling wildly for the prizes, bruises and bloody noses notwithstanding. A fickle dancer named Maurice, after inspecting the Grove's stage floor, successfully demanded that it be covered in black velvet for his inaugural performance.

By fostering such antics, the Cocoanut Grove succeeded in creating an international showcase for the elite of Hollywood's burgeoning kingdom—its first "Playground of the Stars." Whereas entertainment in the past had been much more of local interest, the Cocoanut Grove gave Hollywood a first-class nightspot, a place to be on display, not in country suburbs or roadhouse lanes but right in the middle of swank L.A.

Meanwhile, all over Los Angeles similar spots popped up to compete for the stars' dollars and limelight. The Cinderella Rooftop Ballroom was opened in 1922 on Sixth Street by W. E. Kreiter.

39

The Paris Inn, ''In the shadow of City Hall,'' opened on New Year's Eve, 1924.

Below. Paris Inn interior.

Opposite above. Ruth Roland and party at the Plantation Club in 1929.

Opposite below. Raymond McKee's Zululand on Ventura Boulevard was a '20s hot spot out in the country.

The Venice Ballroom continued to offer the thrills and seaside escape for film folk who wanted a less obvious rendezvous, and Hollywood proper was beginning to open up. The mere mention of its name now sent thousands of tourists searching for the movie stars who supposedly roamed the streets, hopping from one party to the next. That reputation, coupled with the town's growth and newfound wealth, made entertainment ventures lucrative. Restaurants like Musso and Frank's and Henry's were the staple star haunts, but in December 1922, Eddie Brandstatter, late of the Sunset Inn and other nighteries, opened the Montmartre Cafe right in the middle of Hollywood. For star attendance, it gave the Cocoanut Grove a run for its money in the 1920s, until the appearance of the Brown Derbys later in the decade. Although it was open in the evening and hosted dance contests with plenty of hot jazz, the Montmartre was better known for its luncheon trade, especially on Wednesdays, which a wise Brandstatter set up for film folk. The restaurant held 350 patrons, and the parade of celebrities who filled the cafe found themselves surrounded by the accoutrements of the privileged—chandeliers from Czechoslovakia, carpets from Brussels, and 2,400 pounds of solid silver service. Meyer and Holler, who built the neighboring Grauman's Egyptian and Chinese theaters, were the architects, and the restrained Romanesque building housed a twenty-four hour delicatessen, also owned by Brandstatter, on street

level. Whatever antics other clubs promoted, the Montmartre certainly followed suit. An amusing luncheon fad developed for some of the female patrons of the club. How long it lasted is uncertain, but it involved the newly popular airplane. "Flying Luncheons" were initiated by Mrs. Jack Maddux, wife of the airplane manufacturer, who hosted a group of cinemites that included Mabel Normand and Mrs. Fatty Arbuckle. After lunch, they would motor to the nearest airfield, where once skybound, the ladies whiled away several hours in the clouds, playing bridge and chatting.

Meanwhile, on the ground, regular Montmartre guests were included at a dinner party for the Marquise De la Falaise De la Coudray (Gloria Swanson, to her fans), hosted by New York's speakeasy prima donna, Texas Guinan. Joan Crawford, when not at the Cocoanut Grove, shimmied up a storm on Montmartre tabletops. Valentino and date Winifred Hudnut shared their meal with her pet pup alongside, the tourists kept at bay by a red velvet rope. The guest book, the first of which was stolen, boasted the silent era's best: Ruth Roland, Mary Philbin, Leatrice Joy, Betty Compsom, Raquel Torres, Bebe Daniels, Dorothy Mackaill, John Barrymore, and Marion Davies. Joining them were visiting notables: Winston Churchill, the King of Sweden, and Prince George of England, all of whom signed the book.

When it temporarily closed in 1929, the Montmartre had more than quenched

41

The Brown Derby at its original Wilshire Boulevard location.

the public's thirst for a place to see their heroes and heroines hard at play, and in surroundings befitting their stature; and although it was reincarnated various times, the Montmartre's zenith had been reached.

Occasionally, other clubs outside Hollywood generated some of the nighttime fanfare the bigger joints usually monopolized. Coffee Dan's, in an alley downtown on Hill between Seventh and Eighth, could count on more adventurous celebs to slide down a chute into the ramshackle interior of a boite straight out of the Latin Quarter. Apache dancers wound around fake boulder pillars in the dim basement light, while ham and eggs were served on rustic tables to the tune of a jazz band. It was a movie set come to life, and show folk loved it. What better way to pass a Prohibition evening than on "the best little wiggle-block in Los Angeles"? In the shadow of City Hall, another downtown nighterie was cashing in on the bohemian atmosphere of prewar Paris. The Paris Inn had them standing in line to sample Hollywood's version of the Left Bank. Debuting on the last day of 1924, Bert Rovere and partner Innocente Pedroli combined their Italian backgrounds with a penchant for things French and ended up with host Bert belting out arias to customers seated on either the "Bohemian" side or the "Renaissance" side. Singing waiters became a staple, and Bert's guests—from Charlie the Tramp, Clara Bow, and Gary Cooper to Strangler Lewis and the cream of L.A.'s legal system—sat it out while

sketch artists in smocks and berets jotted down caricatures against the painted background of a typical Parisian street scene, with the Eiffel Tower looming romantically in the distance.

Along the same lines, on a stretch of Sunset soon to become "the Strip," La Boheme offered a version of Normandy just as nutty as its downtown counterparts. The well-known feature here was still more tantalizing than getting your portrait sketched. On county land, a good bottle of booze was a sure thing, and the Boheme's cellar was rumored to be well stocked. Who said nightlife had to be fake palms and fancy clothes? If the French look had stars bored, a short trip over the hills to San Fernando Valley promised assorted roadhouses in various styles. The Zulu Hut was a favorite stop for jungle-inspired fun. Half a mile beyond Universal City on Ventura Boulevard, host "Zulu Chief" Raymond McKee and his black-faced waiters dispensed somewhat incongruous cornpones, squab, and fried chicken to those willing to dine over the hill in thatched huts amid orange groves and bean fields.

Other highways proved as fertile for these zany setups. In fact, just about any drive around the Southland netted some kind of oddball drive-ups to enjoy at night. At Pumpkin's, Coffee Pot's, Lighthouses, Indian Pueblos, Chili Bowls, Pigs and Zeppelin's, sandwiches and snacks could be consumed in the privacy of a roadster, where a personal flask complemented dinner. Just as strange in name, but not

43

44

architecturally, Ptomaine Tommy's, on Broadway just north of Chinatown, had celebrities in line for Tommy's creation— a burger patty smothered in chili and onions that he called a "size." Sporting fans usually showed up at the twenty-two seat counter after a hard day at the fights or the polo fields; the elks' heads and a cigar counter dispensed a definitely masculine air. The White Spot, at Wilshire and LaBrea, was another grab-and-chew hamburger stand favored by the movie crowd. When its owner, Cecil Hall, added another location on Beverly Boulevard, he uptowned the interior with oriental rugs and hand-painted tapestries— the better to accommodate the stars who came to eat steak at "the red gum counter set upon a base of lavendar-colored tile."

In spite of the spate of restaurants surrounding filmdom, there were still those who found the food and nightlife not up to par. Enter a group of disgruntled transplants headed by Herbert Somborn (ex-husband of Gloria Swanson), Wilson Mizner (acerbic wit late of Broadway and Boca Raton), and silent third partner Jack Warner. Warner, citing his contemporaries Mary Pickford, Bebe Daniels, Corinne Griffith, and others as having "no really first-class restaurant where actors of lofty eminence could dine in relative privacy," was the financial backer. Somborn had purchased the property just opposite the Ambassador as his contribution. Mizner, recently befriended by Somborn, provided the atmosphere and supplied the name for the new place. Mizner, along

Opposite. An impressive Wilshire Boulevard in 1928. The Brown Derby, flanked by billboards, stands opposite the Ambassador Hotel's entrance.

Below. The Derby's interior.

with the others, had longed for some social focal point that served up good hardy staples, like Jack Dunstan's in pre-Prohibition New York (a Mizner favorite). How the restaurant got its name has as many versions as its menu had items, but it probably derived either from the headgear worn by the two men Mizner most admired—Bat Masterson and Alfred E. Smith—or from Somborn's belief that "You could open a restaurant in an alley and call it anything, if the food and service were good, the patrons would just come flocking. It could even be called something as ridiculous as the Brown Derby."

Whatever the reason, the Brown Derby was constructed to look just like one, and in 1926, it opened to the immense pleasure of nearly everyone in Hollywood. Somborn, a man of impeccable taste, was known as "a connoisseur of what the elite desires," and he made sure that everything that went into his restaurant was of the highest caliber—from the finishing touches on the hamburgers to the hiring of "good lookers" for waitresses (a few of whom were ex-Ziegfeld Follies girls).

The place seated a hundred, and for all its reputation, the interior was almost plain. Booths hugged the walls, and in the center, a counter encircled a service area. Next to the entrance was the cashier, from whom you could obtain gum, cigars, or seats for "theatres, fites and amusements." Above each booth was a signature Derby light fixture. Below the light

45

Opposite. A Derby booth with a signature light fixture.

in Booth 50, Wilson Mizner held court. At the time of the Derby's opening, he had only recently settled in Los Angeles—in the Ambassador, across the street. Hightailing it out of Florida after being implicated in a real estate swindle, Mizner was posing as a millionaire idler and leaning on old friends to provide gainful employment. He landed a job as writer for several studios, and got involved with the Derby. What made him "The Sage of Booth Fifty" was "his colossal gall, his ability to charm, and his social desirability as an informal entertainer and raconteur." With those credentials, he began a seven-year run, lambasting anyone who came through the Derby doors. He informed one studio executive: "You had rubber pockets in your pants so you could steal soup. You were sixty years old before you knew what a bathtub was for. You prove one thing—the marvelous persistency of the uninspired." His tirades against tinsel town were equally vitriolic. Jack Warner recalled a dinner with Douglas Fairbanks, Sr., and Sid Grauman: ". . . Fairbanks grumbled that his table rocked. 'And why not?,' Mizner said. 'How can you expect anything in Hollywood to be on the level?'" Denouncing suckers and chumps most of the night, Mizner also had a soft spot for moochers and borrowers. Usually, by the end of the evening, a wad of bills had disappeared and the evening paper was bought on credit. To help rectify the situation, Mizner had the Derby install one-way glass, so he could see potential

loansharks before they could spot him. His booth was always open to old friends, as well as Hollywood swells. On any given night, he might be host to George Jessel, Mae Murray, Charlie Chaplin, W. C. Fields, Daryl Zanuck, John Barrymore, or Adela Rogers St. Johns. Others might be writers, to one of whom Mizner dished this advice in respect to potential brawlers: "Always hit the man with a catsup bottle. Then he'll think he's bleeding to death." The advice went unheeded one evening when John Gilbert headed for the writer's booth, intent on settling an offensive article with blows. The writer left the catsup bottle on the table, and used his fists to deck Gilbert with one blow. Another fight chalked up in Hollywood annals.

With or without Wilson Mizner, the Brown Derby was a huge success. It edged out the Montmartre as a nighttime dining ritual, and because it was open until 4 A.M. the leftovers from all over town congregated at the Derby. It was said that everyone in Hollywood, with the exception of Greta Garbo, set foot in the Brown Derby. Its legend secure, the Derby started showing up in films and fan magazines. The waitresses' hoopskirts, starched to resemble derbies, became as famous as the stucco building known for its corned beef hash, stew, pot roast, and pie. So confident had it become that it could advertise its food in a like manner: "Our ham sandwiches are made from pleased pigs that have made perfect hogs of themselves."

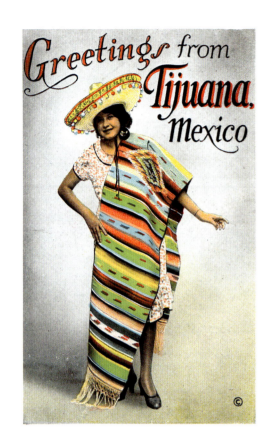

48

*Right. One of Tijuana's early successes,
The Foreign Club featured gambling among
its many delights.*

With so appreciative a public, it was no surprise that Somborn acquiesced in opening another Derby, this time in the heart of Hollywood, on Vine, a half-block south of Hollywood Boulevard. On Valentine's Day, 1929, the second Brown Derby had them in line as no other restaurant in Hollywood could. The same food policy stood: a simple menu, made with the best ingredients. Warner Brothers art director Carl Weyl was architect of the rambling, Spanish-style building, built specifically for the site. Larger by one hundred seats, in its early stage it was one large room, attended by a male-only staff whom Somborn inspected every day for slick shaves, immaculate cuffs, and flawless uniforms. Low-sided booths were built for maximum vision, and although the custom of paging customers and delivering a telephone to their table originated at the Wilshire Derby, it reached high art at the Hollywood version. The caricatures painted on the walls were missing in the early Hollywood Brown Derby but soon artist Eddie Vitch was cranking out walls full of the Derby's most prominent customers, while the maitre d' was in charge of shuffling portraits to insure an ''ex'' wasn't hung next to a ''current,'' and to replace a fallen star with a rising one. The booths were the favored spots for stars to eat, and eventually the north wall front tables were the ones reserved for the heavies. Commoners got the center, and their treat was to watch the famous chow down their food. Wallace Beery ordered the corn beef hash, with catsup-drenched sponge cake for dessert; while Tom Mix, in full Western gear, ate bouillabaisse. Joe E. Brown was another corn beef hash man. June Collyer preferred creamed chicken, and in a corner, Lola Lane, Joan Bennett, and Bebe Daniels might be munching on their favorite—lobster. These newsy tidbits became the fodder fans fed on, and they were supplied to the press by the Derby's public relations firm, headed by Margaret Ettinger, a relative of Louella Parsons (who, coincidentally, made the Vine Derby her home base for dispensing the latest Hollywood gossip.) The Derby's move to employ a p.r. firm was a stroke of genius, and the perpetual vigil of autograph hounds at the front door was testament to a job well done.

The Vine Street Derby was also the embarkation point for Friday night fights at the Hollywood Legion Stadium, a block behind the restaurant. At promptly eight o'clock, the Derby would empty, the throng filing through the parking lot to the ring, to return after the bouts for late-night snacking. For those interested in duking-it-out closer to home, the Derbys were always available battlegrounds, as attested by the number of bloody noses Nick the headwaiter patched up.

The limelight cast on Hollywood's new movie royalty by the Derbys, the Cocoanut Grove, and other nighteries around town was fine when a star's image needed buffing, or a new movie was about to premiere. But when the glow got too hot, a quick retreat was in order, and there

49

OLD MEXICO enchants at the Foreign Club de Luxe, quaint Tijuana's rendezvous for devotees of dining, dancing and diversions.

Julius Rosenfield
Manager

The Foreign Club was where a young Rita Hayworth performed for Hollywood executives.

Opposite above. The Alhambra Cafe was one of the dozens that lined Tijuana's main drag.

Opposite below. Tijuana's Mexicali Beer Hall, boasting ''The Longest Bar in the World.''

were a couple of nearby escapes furnishing Jazz Age hi-jinks in less visible surroundings.

Mexico was too close to ignore in view of the sad state Prohibition imposed on Hollywood imbibers. True, illegal booze wasn't difficult to obtain with the right connections, usually a fat billfold, but how much nicer it was to enjoy one's vices uninhibited, and out of the country to boot. Tia Juana, as it was dubbed then, was a scant two hours away by automobile, and wide open. Since 1889, Tia Juana was known as a magnet for tourists, but for years it remained a collection of shacks, most of which were saloons. It took fight promoter ''Sunny Jim'' Coffroth to actually get things rolling, when he joined a group of investors, the Baja California Investment Company, and proceeded to open up a racetrack, which was also forbidden in California. The Tijuana Fair, a promotion that had opened in conjunction with San Diego's 1915 Panama Exposition, was the border town's first major attraction, and though it was supposed to be a showcase of Mexicana, the addition of the Monte Carlo—a $10,000 gambling emporium—had tourists scrambling across the desolate border. The actual opening of the racetrack was on January 1, 1916, and on hand were 10,000 spectators, including Hollywood notables Eddie Foy and Mack Sennett. The addition of Baron Long to the investment group cemented the Hollywood connection, and those celebrities who patronized the Ship, Vernon Country Club, and other

15499.   Alhambra Cafe,
Tijuana, Mex.

Long hotspots knew they could count on the Baron to show them a good time. By the end of the track's first season, closing ceremonies were attended by Charlie Chaplin and Mabel Normand in front-row seats.

Rumors of opium dens, bandits, gambling, and prostitution did little to diminish Hollywood's fascination with its border Babylon. Whole sections of the town burned down and were quickly rebuilt. The racetrack sailed down the Tijuana River during one flood, but it never missed a season. About the only thing to stop the flow of nightly revelry was the intrusion of World War I, and the closure of the border by the Federal government. By the time Armistice and Prohibition had arrived, Baron Long had constructed the Sunset Inn, a $20,000 extension of the Monte Carlo, where roulette wheels were the draw and croupiers wore evening clothes.

To get to the border track, merrymakers had to pass the Inn, and the gambling hall made a fortune. The Gold Room, built to accommodate high rollers, specifically Universal Studio president Carl Laemmle, was also a favorite of studio head Joseph Schenck, who would motor south in his chauffeur-driven limousine (he in the front with the driver, and wife Norma Talmadge in back with her French teacher) to drop $100,000 on a single race. Fatty Arbuckle, before his fall from grace, partied in two private train cars on his way to the races. And Charlie Chaplin, heading north from Ti-

51

The bawdy frontier atmosphe

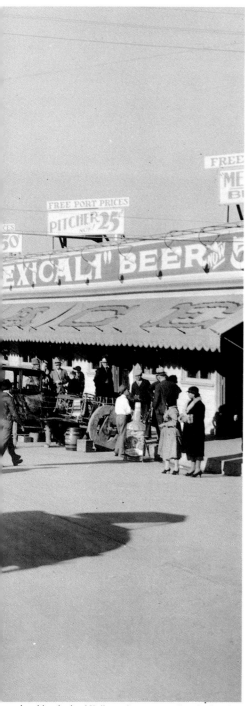

...ana lured hundreds of Hollywood stars to its freewheeling dens.

juana in his Locomobile, was once stopped by a San Diego policeman who warned him about speeding—whereupon Chaplin flagged down a plane flying his friend Jack Pickford back to L.A. The plane landed close enough for Chaplin to climb in and fly off, waving to the law and marooned friends, whom he invited to meet him at the Athletic Club at seven.

Other attractions for the thirsty set were spread along the main drag of town. A reporter from *The Saturday Evening Post* described mid-'20s Tijuana this way: "The drinkers slowly making the rounds . . . starting at the Last Chance Saloon at one end of Main Street, and proceeding through the Cantina Vernon, the Savoy Cafe, the Log Cabin Bar, the Nuevo Palacio, the Tivoli Bar, the Anchor Bar, Booze's Place, the Red Mill, and so on. . . . From every saloon on Main Street come the hectic strains of a jazz orchestra or a jazz piano. In the doorways of the dingier and smaller saloons on the side streets stand little clumps of somewhat underdressed ladies who lure the passerby with honeyed words." The liquor situation wasn't any better. "The local beer is what is technically known as green beer, and frequent indulgence in it is apt to result in an internal upset similar to that which might be caused by swallowing a lighted pinwheel. . . . The science of blending alcohol with creosote, concentrated beet juice, and faucet water has reached such a high stage of development on the North American continent that the drinks of Tijuana seldom cause death if

taken in moderation." Still they came. Tom Mix, Buster Keaton, and Lew Cody were honorary judges at one Jockey Club race. John Gilbert married Leatrice Joy there. Kid star Jackie Coogan was once a guest, and every opening day brought caravans of stars to gamble and drink. Mary Astor, Carmel Myers, Bessie Love, Mary Philbin, Hal Roach, Harold Lloyd, Norma Shearer, Jack Dempsey, and Clara Bow bumped through the muddy streets in Rolls Royces, ending up at the posher places such as the California Club, or the San Francisco, whose owner, Eddie Baker, greeted guests wearing a "chocolate brown suit with daring white stripes, a straw Homberg hat, and a vivid orange tie." The Foreign Club, opened in the summer of 1927, was another big draw. O. O. McIntyre, a syndicated columnist, wrote of it: "The Foreign Club, a handsome new structure, is the biggest gambling house in Tijuana, at the end of Main Street, with acres of parking space. This holds several thousand people, and roulette, fan tan, chuck-a-luck, chemin de fer, black jack, slot machines, and such flourish. There are bars on all four sides of the room to stimulate customers and perk them over their losses. Crowds are orderly, and a violent squawker finds himself being escorted over the line by Mexican guards. . . . I am told the average loss of daily visitors runs twenty dollars a head."

Agua Caliente, the border's biggest resort, opened in 1926, and it really grabbed the film colony. Deluxe accommo-

53

dations now allowed them to spend days or weeks soaking in assorted spas and swimming pools. The Salon de Oro casino permitted gambling only with gold pieces—which was fitting in a place with gold-leafed ceilings and gilt furnishings. The elaborately tiled grounds encompassed exclusive shops, a golf course, tennis courts, bungalows, and a dog-racing track. The Jockey Club, which replaced the old racetrack, held 50,000 to the former's 15,000. Nightlife flourished, complete with bands, Mexican serenaders, and cabaret acts. One Margarita Casino, eluding child labor laws in Los Angeles, performed at the hotel and caught the eye of sojourning Hollywood executives, who, later in Hollywood, transformed her into Rita Hayworth.

Tijuana was always tantalizing, but at times the distance and risk could be burdensome. Other illicit pleasures could be found closer to home. In fact, a mere three miles offshore in the Pacific, a mini-armada drifted between Long Beach and Santa Monica, hawking its wares as blatantly as the Tijuana barkeeps. Gambling ships off the coast first appeared in Long Beach in 1928, when a refitted lumber bark was transformed into a floating casino called the *Johanna Smith*.

Above. Entrance to the Lower California Jockey Club, with the famed gambling halls Monte Carlo and Sunset Inn.

Left. Tijuana Race Track.

Baja California's famed resort, Agua Caliente.

Utilizing what amounted to a loophole in the law, gambling was allowed outside the three-mile limit of California's jurisdiction because no Federal law prohibited it. True, no alcohol was supposed to be on board, but the gambling certainly was, despite the city fathers of Long Beach, who tried with all their power to rid their righteous community of the evil doings at sea. The water taxis used to transport customers to and from the ship were seized on the grounds they transported citizens to places where ''immoral acts'' were being committed. But the same could be said of the carriers to Tijuana or Nevada. So, back went the taxis to the *Johanna Smith*, which was soon joined by a fleet of others. Into the bay slipped the *Monfalcone*, the *City of Panama*, the *Monte Carlo*, the *Texas*, the *Showboat*, and the *Caliente*, laying anchor up and down the coast. One ''whoopee'' ship, the S.S. *Playa*, cruised six hours to nowhere until it was twelve miles out, beyond Federal jurisdiction. Then the bar opened and the fun started. Going one step further, the *Playa*'s restaurant even featured out-of-season game that was forbidden stateside. Rival gangs, bootleggers, bandits, and the law kept the ships on the move for the better part of a decade. But in 1929, other events were about to eclipse any seafaring villainy.

55

THE THIRTIES

The new decade really started in the minds of most people when the stock market crashed on Black Friday, October 21, 1929. In 1927, the era of the "silents" came to an end when Warner Brothers introduced Vitaphone, their sound process, and Al Jolson hailed from the screen: "Say Ma, listen to this!" Studio heads were more or less dependent on bankers, and Wall Street called the shots to the former independents. Stars' salaries had skyrocketed, and the machinations of star buildup and the studio system fueled a giant film industry turning out countless productions for an insatiable public. As stars of the silent era were dethroned, they were quickly replaced by others who could "project" by virtue of stage training or the luck of having been born with quality vocal chords. The mansions along Hollywood Boulevard and those near downtown L.A. were abandoned for the privacy of Beverly Hills, Bel Air, and Malibu. The unhampered lifestyle would disappear forever, under the scrutiny of the Hays Office, the Legion of Decency, and overzealous fans. The jazz age of careless sex, drugs, murders, and crime surrendered to the age of GLAMOUR, and to the tidy packaging of a town without wrongdoing. The first years of the Depression were hardly noticed in Hollywood. Sound had flooded filmdom with plenty of new dough, and the courtesans of the camera now in the forefront knew how to spend it.

Hollywood continued to add and drop nightspots according to fashion or popularity. The Brown Derbys clearly established themselves rock solid, and to be a star in '30s Hollywood meant an appearance at one of them, or you really hadn't made it. Herbert Somborn attempted to branch out with his Derby formula by opening briefly a snooty cafe in the "modern style" on Wilshire. Called the Hi-Hat, it was a stone's throw from his original "hat." For the first couple of years into the decade, Zabayon au Porto and Escargot Bourguignone traded places with Somborn's corned beef and hash served at the Derbys. The copper doors and Zenitherm block entrance gave the place a touch of class, but Somborn saw the writing on the wall in 1931 when he declared: "Unless something happens over at the Hi-Hat pretty soon, I'm going to change its name to the Opera Hat so it won't be so hard to fold up." A name change wasn't necessary, for it soon expired, and in its place a newcomer, Perino's, opened up shop.

The Cocoanut Grove's popularity couldn't be leashed, and the club continued headlong as Hollywood's stellar attraction. At the beaches, Venice and Ocean Park were a bit tawdry and not as fashionable, and out in Culver City, Sebastian's continued to pack 'em in. The Plantation had folded, but plenty of illegal mischief was available at the Midnight Frolics ecdysiast exhibitions and at the Sneak Inn, further down on Washington Boulevard.

The Ship continued with some success, but Nat Goodwin's changed hands, be-

Jean Harlow and William Powell enjoy a night out at the Brown Derby.

58

Toshia Mori, Allen Dinehart, and Neozelle Brittone enjoy some risqué Frolics entertainment.

The Frolics on Washington Boulevard in Culver City.

coming the Crystal Pier Bath and Surf Club, featuring nude sunbaths for men and women. The Sunset Inn disappeared, along with Baron Long's other enterprises, to be reincarnated in Tijuana and Agua Caliente, where his interest now lay.

The top draw in the early 1930s, the one that gave the Derbys a run for their money, was Eddie Brandstatter's Embassy Club. Housed next door to the Montmartre on Hollywood Boulevard, the Embassy put-on-the-ritz for a very select number of celebrities. The maximum of three hundred members represented the cream of Hollywood, and officers of the club were headed by Rupert Hughes, Charlie Chaplin, and Antonio Moreno. On the Board of Directors sat Marion Davies, Gloria Swanson, Bebe Daniels, Betty Compson, Norma Talmadge, Constance Talmadge, John Gilbert, King Vidor, and Sid Grauman. Designed by Carl Weyl (who also did the Vine Street Derby), the exclusive club cost nearly $300,000, and was an "artistic blend" of Spanish and Byzantine. Featured was a rooftop promenade and lounge, glass-enclosed, granting its members a sweeping view of the Hollywood Hills. The interior, designed by Mr. and Mrs. D. H. Gardner Soper, was in the modern mode—a new crystal lighting effect was its novel distinction. At the opening in early 1930, ermine was the password. Gloria Swanson slid into the club in a long, close-fitting black satin gown, held up by ropes of rhinestones.

Fans mob Douglas Fairbanks, Sr., at the Hollywood Brown Derby.

Eager autograph hounds in front of the Hollywood Brown Derby.

Corinne Griffith showed up in a similar frock, hers being an empire model of gold chiffon. In fact, on opening night, Howard Greer, fashion doyen, had supplied seven ladies with identical black gowns. Competition was stiff at first. Mary Pickford, who was throwing a party for Lady Mountbatten, lost out in booking the club to Corinne Griffith, who bid first to entertain 150 of her guests for the entire night. But the nighttime interbreeding without an ogling public was boring, and the new place became just a passing fancy. Forced into bankruptcy, Brandstatter opened the doors to the public a year later, and though fan magazines assured readers that Jean Harlow ''danced there on most any night,'' the place never took off, and Brandstatter moved on to other business propositions.

Gambling and bootlegging were still the rage, with Repeal just a breath away. Even the fan magazines were privy to the fact that ''gambling was rampant in Hollywood . . . the public gambling places reported to be more densely populated than the Montmartre on Wednesday afternoon.'' Lady Luck was pursued in a variety of ways, to suit any size of bankroll— from the gilt interiors on Sunset Boulevard to ramshackle sheds down on Santa Monica Boulevard. Farmer Page, an early casino owner, allowed only men into his place. The Golden Club's policy was coed, but entrance was limited to those in evening dress. Drink and eats, from caviar to illegal champagne, were on the house—provided you dropped the appro-

59

One of Sunset Strip's earliest clubs, the La Boheme stocked a cellar filled with illegal hootch.

priate cash. The newspapers warned of East Coast mobsters looking over L.A. as a nice place to open up operations, given the big money that movies were bringing in. The local police claimed that, despite the widespread rumors, there was more smoke than fire, and, under a corrupt mayor, very little was done to hamper the nightly fun that was illegally going on throughout the city.

West of Hollywood, another part of county land was ripe for development. Following the precedent set by Culver City and Vernon, the parcel of land between Hollywood and Beverly Hills slowly grew into the next logical place for nightspots to spring up. Sunset Boulevard, which was to become synonymous with the essence of Hollywood glamour, had its first nightspot at number 9103—a place called Maxine's, run by a genial host called Popi. When his club opened up, an avocado orchard was nearby, and the western terminus of the street was marked by poinsettia fields. A spot called Magnetic Hill was the only thing tourists were interested in, and nearby hillside property was being developed into a real estate venture called Celestial Heights. In 1924, the land that formed the core of the Sunset Strip began to be developed by the descendents of Victor Ponet, who had purchased 220 acres at the turn of the century. His son-in-law Francis Montgomery, with his brother George Montgomery, initially built four buildings smack in the middle of the Strip in Georgian style—one of which became a

smart dining place called the Russian Eagle. Valentino made it his hangout, but in 1930 it mysteriously burned. The proprietor insisted that it was an accident caused by burning candles on a newly erected altar to its Virgin patroness, but that story changed after several days, and somehow Bolsheviks became responsible. What Bolsheviks were doing on Sunset Boulevard was never clearly explained, but at its new location on Vine Street, the Russian Eagle fared better than at its former site.

The La Boheme occupied a spot three blocks to the west of the Eagle, and replaced it as the latest place to show up after dusk. Outside, it looked like a friendly French roadside saloon, but inside it harbored a gambling operation downstairs. The view from La Boheme was of glimmering lights, remarkable even by Hollywood standards, and a reason why this strip of Sunset became an oasis for nightclubbing.

By most urban standards, the Sunset Strip was still out in the woods. In the early '30s, orchards still clung to the hillside, and there were few sidewalks. But it was the most direct route for stars and industry captains to head home from Hollywood proper to Beverly Hills, and anything that was built along the stretch had to be noticed. Because it was so convenient, agents began to build their offices along the street. Other advantages were cheap rents and lower license fees and taxes. Its reputation, slowly building, would climax when business entrepre-

61

An infant Sunset Boulevard, looking east from Doheny Drive in 1933.

62

The Scandia Restaurant would later occupy the site of Gates' Nut Kettle on Sunset near Doheny.

neur Billy Wilkerson opened his Cafe Trocadero on the site of the old La Boheme in 1934.

In 1930, miniature golf was the rage, and movie exhibitors were berating its popularity for diminishing their revenues. *Cimarron* was on its way to being the best picture of that year, and rising stars Marlene Dietrich, Jean Harlow, Clark Gable, and James Cagney were beginning to be seen at places in Hollywood such as B.B.B.'s Cellar on Cosmo Street, or the Frisky Pom Pom Club on Santa Monica Boulevard. Clara Bow, whose "It" was beginning to wane, once hosted a bash for the winners of the New York-to-Los Angeles air race at the Pom Pom, but its real draw was the bevy of gals "Glorifying Hollywood's Most Beautiful Girls" in its Folies Bergère Revue.

The year's highlight at the club was its Parisian show on New Year's Eve, when visiting celebs were privileged to watch an exact re-enactment of the festivities as they were being produced in Paris. A giant egg, upon the stroke of twelve, was broken by "gay elves and nymphs," whereupon emerged tiny soubrette Maxine Rios who, dressed as a tiny chick, immediately broke into her Mardi Gras dance routine. At the Club New Yorker (formerly the Greenwich Village Cafe, next to the Christie Hotel on Hollywood Boulevard), Marlene Dietrich dined with husband Rudolph Sieber; Jean Malin, owner and host of the club; and fellow European actor Maurice Chevalier, dispelling rumors of her impending mar-

*Above left. Robert Young and wife enjoy an
ice show at the Hollywood Polar Palace.*

*Above right. Ruby Keeler and Al Jolson
Hollywood-nightclubbing in 1933.*

Gloria Shea and Lilia Hyams at the Club New Yorker.

The Club New Yorker was located next to the Christie Hotel at Hollywood Boulevard and McCadden Place.

Opposite. Dick Powell, Mary Carlisle, Adrienne Ames, and Bruce Cabot out on the town.

riage to the newly divorced Chevalier. Gloria Swanson, in her pre-health-food days, was glimpsed having dinner with Lois Wilson and Gene Markey at a famous hamburger stand on Wilshire Boulevard.

When not busy striding the links at one of the Tom Thumb golf courses, the dancing set had plenty of choices around town. The El Patio Ballroom at Vermont and Third was close, and certainly large enough to accommodate the largest of Hollywood parties. Its Spanish motif was completely done over in 1933, when it changed hands to become the Rainbow Gardens. The new owners sought out the talents of one Leo Geasland, artist and electrical engineer, to create a new concept in dancing pleasure called Colortrope. Its novel addition to the nightscene was accomplished by 6,000 different-colored Mazda lightbulbs, which were synchronized to interpret the dance band's music. On the floor, dancers were bathed in orange and yellow when a fox trot played, in red tones for jazz tunes, in pastels for waltzes, and in a rainbow of colors for medleys—hence the dance hall's name. One wonders what the color scheme was the night RKO held a post-premiere party called the King Kong Frolic at the dance resort.

The Blossom Room at the Hollywood Roosevelt was a bit more subdued in tempo and temperament. Across from Sid Grauman's Chinese Theater, it was a smart spot to dance, and had been since it opened in 1927. Its reputation wasn't hampered by the fact that it played host

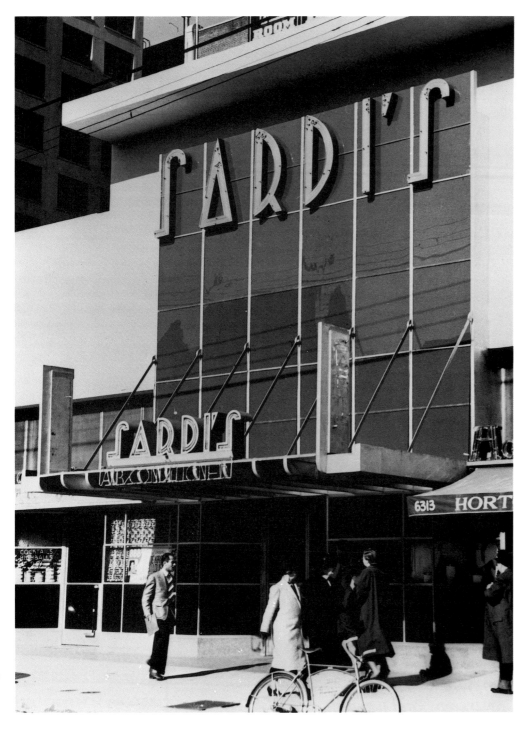

to the first Academy Awards banquet in 1928. For a time, there was even a roof-top garden for outdoor dancing, but the modern-attired ballroom below was the place where the stars held forth.

In 1932, Eddie Brandstatter again opened a cafe directed at the interests of his clientele from former endeavors. Sardi's on Hollywood Boulevard near Vine was a first-class addition to the neighborhood. Designed in the latest architectural mode by architect Rudolph Schindler, the facade had an arresting marquee of sparkling metal and frosted glass, and the restaurant's name spelled out in letter forms also designed by the architect. Like the Montmartre, Sardi's featured daylight dining. Gone were the bands and entertainment, in were the latest interiors and emphasis on a breakfast and luncheon menu, though dinner was also available. A counter to the left of the entrance eschewed stools for counter-height chrome chairs. Beyond the counter section, discreetly separated by a serated stainless steel screen, the main dining room was divided into two levels. Alcoves along the walls were indirectly lit, and each table had a caricature of one of Hollywood's reigning stars. Noiseless hors d'oeuvres wagons plied the aisles at cocktail time, and it was no mistake that a few of the restaurant's features could be found in the Vine Street Derby a stone's throw away. Ever since the Derby stole the Montmartre's business, a friendly though undeclared battle existed between the proprietors, each vying for the other's

The El Patio Ballroom at Vermont Avenue and Third Street.

Opposite. Eddie Brandstatter's ultrasmart Sardi's at 6315 Hollywood Boulevard near Vine Street.

glamorous and wealthy filmdom clientele.

For many of the nightspots, like Hollywood itself, the Depression was just beginning to be felt by 1932. The prosperity produced by the Talkies had ebbed away, and the movie industry was lamenting "hard times." The capricious folding and opening of Hollywood hangouts was already common near the end of Prohibition. Disrupted by raids of local law enforcers, it seemed only a whim that some of the minor clubs hung on. Other places, like the Derby, seemed Depression-proof. Like the movies themselves, shifting from silent to talking pictures, nighttime in cinema city was experiencing a period of transition. Old standbys boarded up their doors, while the new kid on the block soaked up the survivors with the latest novelty or the swankiest decor. A few of the stalwarts bridged the changes, though most everybody in town was anxiously awaiting the legalization of booze—a move that would definitely set a new tone throughout the Southland. Even though some stars, directors, and producers were complaining about their dire financial situations, there were still plenty of others whose pocketbooks never felt the squeeze. The group that frequented the Mayfair Club Balls at the Biltmore, and later on at the Beverly Wilshire and Victor Hugo, seemed immune to any money woes. The private affairs, featuring the cream of Hollywood's crop, were fashioned after similar gatherings in New York and London. The monthly dinner dances were for a

67

68

*The Hollywood Roosevelt's Blossom Room
kicked off '30s glamour.*

*Opposite. Lupe and Johnny, one of the
decade's craziest couples, made the nightclub
scene their second home.*

select 300; the snob appeal of a strictly industry-only affair kept waiting lists long, and cut L.A. society short. At the 1932 New Year's Eve Ball, the highlight of the season, Mexican "Spitfire" Lupe Velez clicked with up-and-coming actor Randolph Scott, and at another Ball later in the decade, Gable and Lombard had their first serious rendezvous. At the December 1933 Ball, the crowded dance floor at the Beverly Wilshire emptied at midnight only to resume at a madcap pace when Gus Arnheim's band took the stage at one A.M. and "things got even better." Carole Lombard and George Raft did the tango while Mary Brian and new crush Russ Columbo looked on. Lupe Velez, draped in rubies, chatted, while a bored Johnny Weismuller sulked. Mary Pickford also displayed a king's ransom in jewels. Others attired accordingly were Bebe Daniels, Ben Lyon, Wes Ruggles, Gloria Swanson, Ernst Lubitsch, Una Merkel, Joe E. Brown, and several hundred others. Press photographers, barred from coming in, threatened to boycott future events. The press boys wanted a peek at the intimate doings of Hollywood after Repeal, but the Mayfair directors said "no dice," and held their ground. For those shutterbugs who stayed on, pictures of tuckered-out stars could be had until predawn hours, as the revelers drifted out of the hotel.

The year Prohibition was repealed, 1933, started out with a bang. In the depths of the Depression, Hollywood was in a quandary about the popularity of its

Mr. and Mrs. Edward G. Robinson,
Ruth Roland, and friend at the
Colony Club.

Opposite. The Nikabob at 9th and
Western was a high-class addition to the
Wilshire district.

product. Attendance had taken a down-swing, and layoffs at the studios darkened moods in many quarters of cinema city, which gave all the more reason to pack up one's troubles and let loose at the local hot-cha palaces. New Year's Eve saw the opening of Sunset Strip's "newest and smartest cafe," the Club Ballyhoo, snuggled against the hills at Number 8373. Owner Frank Hanofer enticed patrons to his club with opening night entertainment from Eddie South and his International Orchestra, the "musical toast of Europe." In addition, a revue and dinner was included in the five-dollar tab. Down the street, a block south of the Boulevard, Buddy Fisher's Hollywood Barn at Sunset and Cahuenga had opened a couple of days prior to the New Year. There, Buddy Fisher and his Great Band initiated festivities, along with Lester Montgomery's Barnyard Frolics Revue, featuring Hannah, the Prize Cow, Foster's Animal Circus, and the Crocket Mountaineers—radioland's Great Rural family. (The Barn's structure would ten years hence serve as one of Hollywood's most frequented night spots—the Hollywood Canteen). Down Culver City way, Les Moore's New Frolics on Washington Boulevard extended the celebration for two days past New Year's Eve, and again, for five bucks, a somewhat naughty showcase of showgirls pranced for the revelers all night long, with a breakfast for the survivors. Frank Sebastian, as always, packed them in on the same avenue with his multi-roomed dance emporium, to the

71

72

tunes of Les Hite. The frolicking continued out into the Pacific on the gambling ships *Monte Carlo* and *Johanna Smith*. The ''World's Largest Pleasure Ship'' induced partakers daily in the newspapers to follow the neon arrow on the dock and join them for a free dinner and a chance at winning some Depression money on the ''high seas.'' Back on land in Long Beach, on the ''Pike,'' the annual money scramble was more a spectator sport for stars disembarking from the gambling barges than a participatory event, but it provided great fun just the same.

Nursing the effects of its yearly binge, Hollywood entered the year just about the same as it left the old one. Wallace Beery and chum Richard Arlen continued partying at La Boheme, where ''Hollywood Parade,'' the current floor show, was about to make way for the new ''Technocracy Blues'' revue. Howard Hughes, Gilbert Roland, and Connie Bennett returned from Caliente. Katharine Hepburn entertained a party of five at the Brown Derby, while Joan Crawford and Franchot Tone sat nearby, enjoying lunch. New Yorker Jimmy Durante began a run at the Beverly Wilshire, and Hollywood pretty much went about its business.

By springtime, the nest of gambling goings-on began to be stirred up again. Moralists roused by Mae West's *She Done Him Wrong* went looking for victims, and Hollywood's long-standing reputation as vice capital made the nightspots an obvious target for cleanup. The

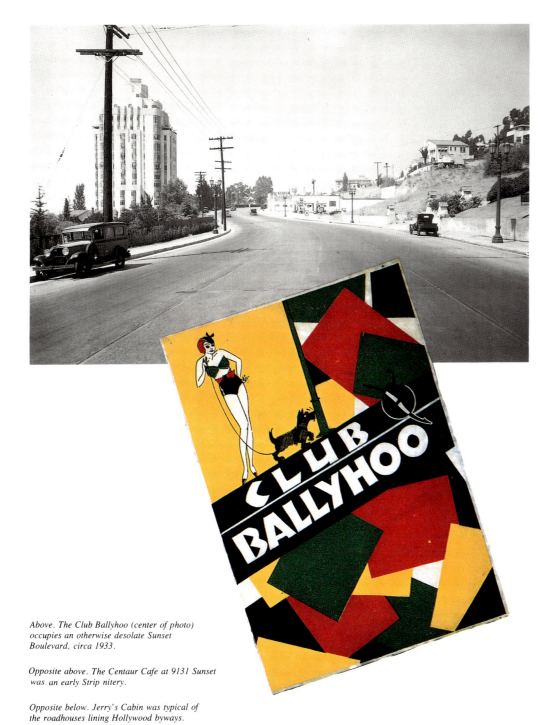

Above. The Club Ballyhoo (center of photo) occupies an otherwise desolate Sunset Boulevard, circa 1933.

Opposite above. The Centaur Cafe at 9131 Sunset was an early Strip nitery.

Opposite below. Jerry's Cabin was typical of the roadhouses lining Hollywood byways.

result was a series of raids by local law enforcers throughout the year that made great front page copy in the daily papers but ultimately little or no difference to club owners, who would rely on greased palms to ease the situation. In May, vice-raiders descended on "The Barn" at 6426 Sunset and arrested several waiters for the illegal sale of beer. But as the press noted, " 'The Barn' features a floor show in which men masquerade as women, and women pose as men," which may have been the real target of the raid (particularly since permits for beer sales had been issued since April). At the Back Yard, another Hollywood cafe, more female impersonators were taken into custody at the Hollywood police station and given six-month jail sentences. Also complaining to the law were bar owners on a stretch of Santa Monica Boulevard just south of Sunset. It seems that underworld types were offering protection at fifteen dollars a month to insure that beer was delivered without its somehow getting highjacked en route.

The subtle presence of Eastern racketeers didn't prevent other entrepreneurs from joining in the entertainment and restaurant business, even in the depths of the Depression. Billy Wilkerson, owner of Hollywood's industry tabloid *The Hollywood Reporter*, threw his hat in the ring the first week of May 1933, when he opened The Vendome. It was the first of a string of highly successful and visible restaurant–nightclubs to grace Hollywood's night scene. Conveniently located

73

The Vendome and bar occupied 6666 Sunset Boulevard, opposite owner Billy Wilkerson's Hollywood Reporter.

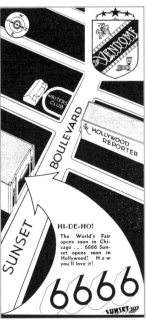

a stone's throw from the *Reporter*'s offices, The Vendome, at 6666 Sunset, was originally planned as a gourmet paradise and specialty store for Hollywood's royalty. Full-page ads in the *Reporter* announced with regularity the parade of foodstuffs that were stocked on the shelves, arriving by boat, plane, and train. Goose livers in cans, Westphalian ham from Germany, Yarmouth bloaters, large gray-egged Russian caviar from pedigreed sturgeon, Edam in Sauterne, brandied fruits, "smoky" teas, and an endless procession of delights were offered for the daily customers of "the royalty of the screen" profession.

Unable to resist the chance to serve his patrons, Wilkerson initiated luncheon at The Vendome, and almost immediately it became the most important place to lunch in town. A significant factor in its success was that select members of the film community dining at a Wilkerson establishment could rest assured that their name would be mentioned in the gab columns the following day. Within a month, the paper was informing its readers of the social roll call visiting The Vendome. Countess Dorothy Di Frasso is credited with commencing the social whirl there when she threw a costume ball with an English motif, no doubt to complement the establishment's large stock of Fortnum and Mason products. The Countess, actually an East Coast divorcée who married into the title, was arbiter for the social set, and a party thrown by her indicated general approval of the establishment.

75

Opposite. The Hofbrau Garden at 6361 Sunset was one of the first clubs to serve pre-Repeal beer.

Fan magazines and gossip columns were filled with the names of the stars who crossed The Vendome's threshold. Typically, a lunch crowd might consist of Mae West, Joan Crawford, the Gables, Louella Parsons, and Marlene Dietrich. At one luncheon, Louella picked up what she considered the scoop of her career, when Mary Pickford confided her impending divorce from Douglas Fairbanks—which Louella discreetly unfolded in banner headlines.

To bolster his creation, Wilkerson continued his advertising campaign, even going so far as to explain the crest of the restaurant. Its highfalutin imagery included a mounted knight, a mailed hand holding a silver goblet (both recalling the historic period in which Fortnum and Mason began), and, of course, a strip of film celluloid and a band of stars signifying good old modern-day Hollywood.

Elsewhere around town, other places started popping up, most of them offering beer when it was finally legal. The Hofbrau Gardens opened in June on Sunset near Vine, and was a full-fledged beer garden with dirndl-skirted waitresses and an oom-pah-pah band. Owner Carl Ziegler was Swiss, though the prevailing atmosphere was strictly German—a point that was carefully dodged given the political developments of the times. Thus the restaurant was described as Viennese with Swiss Influence. Inside, the illusion of outdoors was accomplished by a ceiling covered with tree branches and hanging birdhouses, and strung with lights.

Collections of steins littered shelves, and Swiss chalets jutted out from the walls, through whose windows murals of Alpine peaks were visible. Wandering in off the street, patrons would hardly be surprised if someone shouted "action" and cameras whirred—so closely did the place resemble a set. But the novelty clicked, and stars made a beeline for the saurbrauten, Koenigsberger klops, badisher hecht, and apple kuchen prepared by master Swiss chef John Cley. Headwaiter Albin Graf, a devoted nudist, would seat guests at one of the checker-clothed tables, initiating their journey into Bavarian giddiness. Finishing a hearty meal, diners were free to dance, and, when leaving, they were exhorted to hurry back by the cafe's motto: "To the happy, one time means nothing."

During the summer, such successful releases as *Dinner at Eight* bolstered Hollywood's self-image, and the town was in the mood to play. The Brown Derby was lampooned in the prologue of the premiere for *Gold Diggers of 1933* at Grauman's Chinese Theater, where, earlier, a parade of chorines had wound their way from Warner Brothers studio on Sunset to the theater. If the Depression was at its height, it was hard to tell from the queues at Lucca Restaurant at Fifth and Western. The lines weren't for soup and bread, but for Italian dinners—246,000 of which the restaurant had served to Angelenos and resident personalities who mingled with the populace during the first five months of operation. Here, the

77

78

slogan "Where dull care is forgotten" meant dancing to jazz tunes during the week. On Sunday afternoons, operatic fans could drown their problems and down their ravioli to the talents of 100 artists broadcasting live on Hollywood station KNX. But bit players weren't the only ones waiting in line. Immensely popular Maurice Chevalier was kept waiting at Sardi's for half an hour by his luncheon date, who apologetically turned up, but not before the impropriety was noted.

Also keeping tabs on the stars' goings-on were members of the W.C.T.U. and local clergy. Declaring that never had Los Angeles been so wide open for prostitution, liquor, and gambling in its history, the irate watchdogs were demanding a closer look at the Colony Club, where the playing of games of chance was routinely reported in the city's news columns. Such respected stars as Gary Cooper, Kay Francis, Jean Harlow, Lillyan Tashman, and the Countess Di Frasso rolled dice with relative ease and seemingly little concern for the somewhat illegal nature of their play. The resulting furor caused a series of raids through the remainder of the year, and brought enough pressure to close the West Hollywood branch, which reopened in Culver City on Motor Avenue, adjacent to the Hillcrest Country Club.

By summer's end, several deaths were a reminder of the film colony's good old days. Texas Guinan, the queen of New York night clubs, died in Vancouver; and,

Opposite. The Three Little Pigs at 335 N.
LaBrea borrowed Walt Disney's popular
characters for its identity.

closer to home, the death of Fatty Arbuckle, the perennial cutup of early
Hollywood, closed the era's unchecked
nightlife.

Another subtle reminder of the changing face of Hollywood was the reopening
of the once-fashionable Embassy Club
by Ernie Primm, who rechristened the
structure on Hollywood Boulevard the
Edgemont Club, in October 1933. Other
new additions to the nightscene—which
opened and closed with such frequency
that patrons almost needed a guide to
find out the current name of a club—
included the Hermitage on Hollywood
Boulevard, which billed itself as ''a
Rendezvous for Film Folk''; the Three
Little Pigs Beer Garden on LaBrea near
Beverly Boulevard, which lifted the name
from Walt Disney's highly successful car-
toon of that year; and the King's Club,
located in the hills above Sunset Strip,
which flung its doors open in October,
and later moved to Sunset on the site of
the Centaur Club.

Also that year, one of the most prominent ''private'' clubs ever to exist on
Sunset Boulevard opened where La Cienega ended at Sunset. Reached by a
large ramp, and literally built on the side
of a hill, the Clover Club was one of
Hollywood's most exclusive and re-
nowned night spots. Admission was by
membership, which usually meant that
either you had the money or the right
face to pass the threshold. For those who
did pass the doorman's muster, an evening
of gambling and the best in dining and

79

Above. Enjoying the Clover Club are Reginald Gardner and Margaret Graham.

Opposite. The Clover Club, one of Hollywood's most famous clubs, was located where LaCienega ended at Sunset Boulevard.

entertainment were for the asking. Almost instantly it was a hit, and continued to be so until a reform administration finally closed its doors five years later.

As the liquor laws changed, many of these exclusive clubs—more correctly dubbed ''speaks'' by the local trade papers—verged on respectability, and could be mentioned on radio programs. The clubs got free advertising in the form of live broadcast time, with music coming live from this or that ''exclusive'' club. Those in the know knew what ''exclusive'' meant in this case. The change of heart, the papers reasoned, hinged on the ''current liberal attitude on liquor and gaming tables, and lack of any regulations against liquor selling.'' So light-handed was legal action that one ''speak'' posted the regulation NRA sign indicating a closing time of 4 A.M. along with another, saying: ''After 4, patrons must knock.''

By November, the stars seemed to be heading out nightly to be seen and sample some of the wares at all the new hot spots. The *Hollywood Reporter* revealed record business, especially at the Colony Club and the Clover, where customers had to be turned away for lack of space in both parking lot and interior. At the two clubs one weekend were Fay Wray, fresh from the arms of King Kong, escorted by Johnny Mack Saunders; the Laemmles, Junior and Senior; Mervyn LeRoy; David Selznick; and Gregory Ratoff.

Flushed out of the West Hollywood

81

82

Above. Robert Cummings and date sign autographs outside the Hollywood Brown Derby.

district, the Colony Club reopened on Motor Avenue in another "free" area of Culver City. Not about to lose a penny, the club briskly opened in mid-November, under the direction of two gentlemen with dubious pasts. Al Wertheimer and Bob Goldie greeted guests in a place formerly called the Palomar Club, and it seemed that every member of the Hollywood gambling crowd followed them there for opening night. Al Wertheimer, recently of Detroit, where he was involved in another club called the Colony, had been instrumental in opening a gambling joint a week before called the Dunes in Palm Springs, a more distant outpost favored by the stars. The moniker "Purple Gang" always seemed to follow Wertheimer and his brother Lou, though mob connections didn't seem to bother the more than three thousand picture folk who turned out for the Culver City branch opening. Local residents, however, were bothered, annoyed by the noise, traffic, and obviously undesirable element that was setting up shop in their backyards. Within days, complaints initiated another round of raids in Culver City and the surrounding Southland. Among those hit by order of Sheriff Eugene Biscailuz was the La Casa Madrid on DeLongpre in West Hollywood, where four hundred patrons watched gaming tables seized and management arrested "to the strains of 'The Last Roundup' as played by a colored orchestra." Among the guests were "fashionably gowned motion picture actresses and their tuxedo-clad escorts, as well as society matrons out on a lark.'' Abatement notices were served at the recently opened Club Ballyhoo and at Al Freitas's Club Seville, both on the Strip. Heading out to the hinterlands, the deputies continued their raids at the Barn in Altadena and at the Du-Dillon Club in Watts, where ''guests left waiting autos and fled over backyards and fields.''

The warnings unheeded, stars turned out en masse two nights later, jamming the roulette tables at the Colony. Connie Bennett, who seemed to be out nightly, won a tidy sum, cheered on by fellow stars Wes Ruggles, Adolphe Menjou, Thelma Todd, the Selznicks, and the evening's centerpiece, Clara Bow, attired in bright green dress, flaming red hair, orange gloves, and a mass of rhinestone buckles.

The much-anticipated Repeal finally took place on November 7. The expected overindulgence failed to materialize, but in the spirit of things the stars turned out to celebrate the resurrection of John Barleycorn. For those celebs intent on partying on the wilder side, Main Street in downtown Los Angeles was the scene of dancing in the streets, with locals guzzling booze in record amounts. For those with the money and access to private clubs, a more subdued evening was in store, perhaps prompted by the intense eye of the media. Everyone from the President on down was requesting moderation, and the stars pretty much conformed to the unspoken rules of propriety. The town's clubs, restaurants, and enter-

83

Above. William Gargan, Joan Blondell, and Hugh Herbert.

Below. At Club Airport Gardens, Prohibition's demise lasted four fun-filled days.

84

Above. Ads for the Century Club, noted for its gambling, and the Ballyhoo, noted for its rowdiness.

Opposite. The bar at the Biltmore Lounge.

tainment spots, however, could hardly be expected to restrain this welcome break from the Depression. At the Beverly Wilshire Hotel, in the Gold Room, Gus Arnheim played to the celebrating crowd at a "Victory Celebration of the peoples' victory over prohibition and the repeal of the Eighteenth Amendment." The direct election returns from the six deciding states were broadcast to inform partygoers of the final countdown to Repeal. At The Vendome, an all-night party, under the guise of a "New Year's celebration," was underway. Down the street, the Colony and the Clover were packed, the Clover being the favorite of Raoul Walsh, Ben Lyon, and the Junior Laemmles. Over in Glendale near the new airdrome, Club Airport Gardens drew the crowds for four nights to announce the "Death of Prohibition." Owner Tommy Jacobs, of Ship Cafe fame, was head mortician for the joyous funeral ceremonies. The hubbub the clubs created with or without the legalization of booze was still fuel for nearby residents of some of the noisier clubs, and the do-gooders pressured the law enforcers to tighten the screws once more. So, in the first part of December, the lawmen descended once again into the dark domains of rum and roulette, and slapped hands to keep face. The Colony Club in Culver City was becoming the focal point for irate neighbors, who, once they realized more than a friendly game of bridge was going on, harassed the club and eventually forced it to move on to less scrutinized grounds.

But on the night of the raid, in what would normally be a beehive of activity, raiders only found a Filipino houseboy and a night watchman, in addition to a large quantity of silent gambling equipment. The Embassy on Hollywood Boulevard was also raided, and a new place, the Club Seville, in the 8400 block of Sunset, found its doors momentarily locked.

The nightclub raids made small news, however, alongside the bombshell laid on Hollywood when Doug and Mary announced their divorce on December 9, 1933. To the press, the misdeeds of a few clubs were nothing compared to what amounted to a royal breach of promise. Reeling from that news, the filmites began preparations for the New Year and brighter prospects. One movie hit of the season, *Little Women*, premiered at Grauman's with most of the first-nighters heading for the Colony for a post-party drink. Another group of stars were planning their own shindig for entry into the New Year. Connie Bennett, Henri de Falaise, George Cukor, Ernst Lubitsch, Lewis Milestone, Gary Cooper and new bride Sandra Shaw, the Cedric Gibbons (Dolores Del Rio), and a bunch more arranged to take over one of the local "speaks" for a private party with "a couple of orchestras and entertainers thrown in." The rain that night dampened a few celebrants, but, for those who took off for Caliente, the gambling south of the border warmed up spirits. Sighted in the border resort were Raoul Walsh, Bruce

85

Above. The Johanna Smith, where illicit fun was a mere three miles offshore.

Opposite. The Biltmore Bowl boasted an unobstructed view of the dance floor and was the showpiece of the downtown hotel when it opened on April 5, 1934.

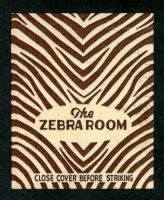

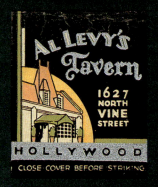

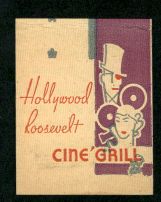

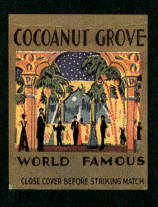

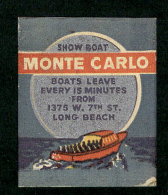

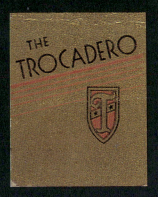

THE
TROCADERO

PERINO'S
RESTAURANT

UNEXCELLED
CUISINE and
SERVICE

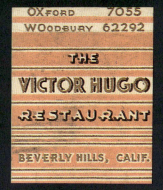

OXford 7055
WOodbury 62292

THE
VICTOR HUGO
RESTAURANT

BEVERLY HILLS, CALIF.

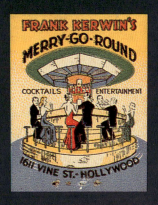

FRANK KERWIN'S
MERRY-GO-ROUND
COCKTAILS · ENTERTAINMENT

1611 VINE ST · HOLLYWOOD

Phone HO. 6311

FLORENTINE
Gardens

Foremost
CABARET
RESTAURANT
in America

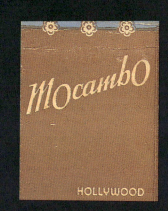

MOcambo

HOLLYWOOD

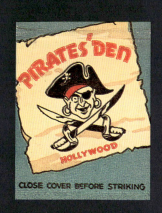

PIRATES DEN

HOLLYWOOD

CLOSE COVER BEFORE STRIKING

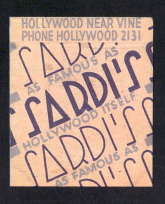

HOLLYWOOD NEAR VINE
PHONE HOLLYWOOD 2131

SARDI'S
AS FAMOUS AS
HOLLYWOOD ITSELF
SARDI'S
AS FAMOUS AS

HOLLYWOOD 700
JITTERBUG
HOUSE · 875 NORTH VINE · Hollywood
CLOSE COVER BEFORE STRIKING

DON THE BEACHCOMBER ®
HOST TO
DIPLOMAT AND BEACHCOMBER,
PRINCE AND PIRATE

MATCH BOOK — LION MATCH CO. INC.

CLUB
U-GENE

COCKTAIL
LOUNGE

WILSHIRE
BOWL CAFE

5665 WILSHIRE
LOS ANGELES

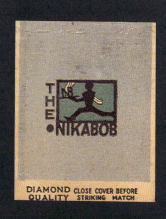

THE
NIKABOB

DIAMOND CLOSE COVER BEFORE
QUALITY STRIKING MATCH

90

Above. A cozy Glenda Farrell and Donald Woods at the Biltmore Bowl.

Cabot, and the nation's heartthrob—Clark Gable. At midnight, several score of women made a beeline for the "King," who obliged tradition and lightly bussed each admirer.

A couple of weeks into 1934, the *Hollywood Reporter* crowed that the city's nightlife was on a roll. In town, to capacity crowds, were the Mills Brothers and Guy Lombardo. At the Clover Club, a few thousand guests were giving Gene Austin a warm welcome. The hoopla that prevailed in almost every American town after Repeal was finally being realized in the movie capital of the world. Certainly not missing a beat in the general up-tempo of the times was the fleet of gambling ships still anchored along the coast. Writer Basil Woon described the scene of the period: "Off Long Beach are several gambling barges and ships, packed nightly with people ferried from the mainland by scores of wasp-like motorboats. Among these ships is the *Rose Isle*. . . . Games played on the gambling ships include chuck-a-luck, roulette, craps, birdcage, stud poker and blackjack. Each ship has two restaurants—a lunch room for losers and an ornate affair with dance floor and orchestra for winners. . . . It doesn't always pay to be a winner on one of these boats. There was one man who, being on the right side of the game to the tune of four hundred dollars, decided to leave. They were all silver dollars, these being the chips used, and he had some difficulty in distributing them about his person.

The bands of Jimmy Griers and Hal Roberts were just a few of the many that initiated the Biltmore Bowl.

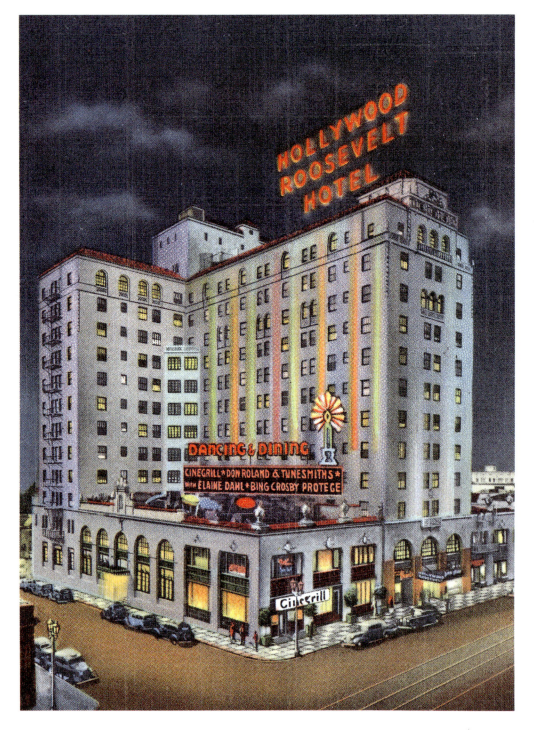

''He succeeded finally, however, and, with silver dollars filling every pocket of his suit and overcoat, boarded the small motorboat for shore. Just outside the harbor, the motorboat collided with another, and every passenger was saved except our hero. He had happened to be the only winner and his dollars had taken him to the bottom and held him there.''

This event, along with heavier gang involvement a few years later, would eventually help to doom the coastal gambling emporiums. But until then, you could bet on a healthy share of the high rollers to be studio heads and their underlings.

Finally flushed out of Culver City, the Colony reopened in March just south of the Strip on Alta Loma Way, in a converted twenty-six-room mansion. The house, built on ten acres, was originally meant to be a replica of an English manor for the owner's homesick British wife. It was a stone's throw from the Clover Club, and several other gambling clubs disguised as homes and hidden in the winding and secluded streets high in the hills, sporting views of the entire city spread out below like a glowing carpet. It was no wonder that the stars preferred to while away the night hours in places with such spectacular backdrops.

The battle to bring the stars out of the hills to the large hotels east of Hollywood began with the venerable Baron Long, who, fresh from Caliente, took over the Biltmore Hotel and christened a brand new entertainment room called the Bilt-

Above. The Circus Bar was conveniently located below the Actors Guild at 6656 Hollywood Boulevard, insuring it a star clientele.

Opposite. The Roosevelt at its mid-'30s zenith.

Above. A stellar group of Hollywoodites, including the Irving Thalbergs, the Robert Montgomerys, and the Clark Gables, gathers at the Cocoanut Grove.

Opposite. Al Levy's, across from the Vine Street Derby, later changed hands and became Mike Lyman's.

more Bowl on April 5, 1934. Employing architect Wayne McAllister, who designed several structures at Agua Caliente, Long had the former Sala de Oro ballroom transformed into the world's largest nightclub. The Bowl was 140 feet long and unobstructed by posts. All the seats, on several levels, commanded perfect views. For each of the 1,200 patrons on opening night, the five-dollar tariff paid for a bottle of French champagne and continuous entertainment featuring Hal Roberts's orchestra. Following the opening, Jimmy Grier and his orchestra headlined, thereby insuring the Bowl's success as a top-rated night spot.

With the stars in regular attendance, the society crowd wanted in, and made the Bowl the spot for their parties. The fraternities and sororities from nearby colleges virtually took it over for Friday Collegian Nights, and local radio station KFI sent out national broadcasts from the instantly popular room. The Bowl was a jump ahead in the Biltmore's silent rivalry with the Ambassador.

Besides the repeal of Prohibition, there was lots more to celebrate in Hollywood in 1934. Kate Hepburn won an Academy Award, Shirley Temple had another hit with *Little Miss Marker*, Jean Harlow and William Powell seemed to be a happy twosome, and the city of Los Angeles celebrated a little-known anniversary: the thirty-second year since the first motion picture was shown at the Electric Theater on Main Street. Stars found plenty of places to drop in for casual, legal

95

96

Chester Morris and Lillian Bond pose for Cocoanut Grove photographers.

imbibing. Spearheaded by the Hofbrau Gardens, outdoor beer patios sprang up like mushrooms wherever the celebs might tread. Across from the Pantages, the Gaiety Cafe opened an al fresco beer parlor, and, downtown, the Bohemian Gardens opposite the old Selig movie zoo was open for outdoor drinking plus a floor show.

The beer garden concept seemed to be a fleeting trend matched only by a new-found form of entertainment—ice hockey games at the Hollywood Winter Garden Ice Palace. Almost all of Hollywood's well-knowns seemed to be heading for one night club or the other, since nightlife got its second wind after New Year's. A typical night, as reported by the various news sources, might include Joan Crawford and Franchot Tone, Lupe and Johnny, the Bruce Cabots, and the Mack Sennets at the Cocoanut Grove. At a crowded King's Club, Ralph Forbes and Kathleen Ardelle could be spotted, while down on Vine Street, in its post-Bolshevik fire locale, the Russian Eagle reported a three-ring atmosphere surrounding the arrival of Fay Wray and John Monk Saunders, followed by Marlene Dietrich and Josef Von Sternberg and Mae West, accompanied by Frank Timmony, her manager. As usual, the Colony and Clover clubs were packed nightly until dawn, and one reporter noticed the rings around Colony Club owner Lou Wertheimer's eyes had diminished down to three.

The sudden influx of pub crawling all seemed to be leading up to the year's

Dick Powell and Mary Carlisle, a happy Grove twosome.

Grand dame of '30s nightclubs, the Trocadero replaced the La Boheme at 8610 Sunset.

premier event in September. Billy Wilkerson, with his nose for success, was no stranger to the activity stirring up west of his successful Vendome. Since the eaterie was principally known for its luncheon trade, Wilkerson sought out a location for a new venture specifically for the night crowd storming the stretch of Sunset between Hollywood and Beverly Hills. According to one account, Wilkerson was scouting for a place to store his stock of vintage libations and happened upon the La Boheme, which had large cellars for that purpose. The Boheme, known for its gambling and liquor violations, folded about the time Wilkerson began storing his cache, and he bought the place with the idea of opening a nightclub above the basement. With his Midas touch, he employed Harold Grieve, decorator to the stars, to renovate the interior in the mode of a smart French cafe, complementing The Vendome and carrying on the tradition of naming his enterprises after Parisian landmarks. The result was the Trocadero, whose birth, like The Vendome's, was anticipated by a series of provocative ads in Wilkerson's *Hollywood Reporter*.

Wilkerson persuaded agent Myron Selznick to host the opening-night party, which was actually a private affair, before the club's official public opening a few nights later. The aftermath of Selznick's bash was given the following account in the *Reporter*: "At least half the town must be recuperating at the moment from the huge and galorious party given by the

100

Myron Selznicks at the Trocadero Satiddy night. Everybody, in his best soup and tucker, was there and stayed indefinitely. There were hours of sipping in the grill before dinner and dancing in the restaurant upstairs. Joe Schenck and Rosie Dolly did rhumbas that were studies in perpetual motion (especially Joe!) but Gene Markey's Carioca remained restrained to the finish. . . . Among the gobs of guests were the Bing Crosbys, the Dick Arlens, Dororthy Parker, Genevieve Tobin, Hobe Irwin, the Sam Goldwyns, the Freddy Astaires, Bill Powell and Jean Harlow, Arthur Hornblow and Myrna Loy, William Wellman and Mrs. W., the W. K. Howards, Hugh Walpole, Lewis Milestone with Helen Vinson, Junior Laemmle, Ida Lupino, Mel Schauer, Jeanette MacDonald, the Neil Hamiltons, Gilbert Roland, Betty Parsons, and Maurice Revnes, who stayed right to the finish (around 5 A.M.) along with the SINGERS. . . . It was one swelegant party, as 'nobody will deny'!''

The official opening of the Trocadero was held a few nights later on September 17, a Monday evening that coincided with the opening of *A Midsummer Night's Dream* at the Hollywood Bowl. Since the Bowl event was a hot ticket in town, a bit of the Troc's opening night ''premiere'' was clipped, but devoted patrons stormed the place after the play, giving it a late-night boost for the gossip columns the following morning. Prior to the evening's events, the sidewalk cafe debuted at three in the afternoon, initiat-

Above. Bob Cummings and companion arrive at the Trocadero.

Opposite. The Troc at its bewitching hour.

Above. The Henry Fondas enjoying a night at the Troc.

Opposite. Ginger Rogers offers Jimmy Stewart a helping hand, while Allen Jones and his wife relax in the Troc's foyer.

A vibrant Ginger Rogers leaving the Troc with escort Alfred G. Vanderbilt.

The Troc interior in 1936.

ing the "West's first genuine Paris side-walk cafe." The formal dinner-dance commenced at eight at a hefty $7.50 per person, which included dinner prepared by Chef des Cuisines Felix Ganio. Greeting guests were hatcheck girls—"perfect soubrettes, with eyelashes and chic caps and sheer lawn aprons and a vast expanse of silk stockings with a general effect about them of being all knees." Those wishing to freshen up with a cocktail could proceed to the far end of the main corridor with its freshly painted scenes of Paris, and descend into the Bar and Grill in the cellar with its somewhat chummy "American Colonial" interior of red and black plaid and hanging copper utensils.

Upstairs, arrivals entered the main dining room, the select being seated by the balcony where the lights of the city could be viewed. Three headwaiters performed this task, and the procession of food that soon arrived might include Breast of Guinea Hen Under Bell, Larded Tenderloin of Beef Forestière, or Vol au Vent of Sweetbreads Toulousaine, complemented by a Chateau de Rayne-Vigneau 1901 for an additional $9.00. Following dinner, not one but two bands were provided for dancing enjoyment—Harl Smith and his Continental Orchestra, and Ramon Littee and His Parisian Tango Orchestra. Among those opening night revelers were—once again—number-one nightclubber Joe Schenck, tangoing this time with Peggie Fears; the Gene Markeys (Joan Bennett); Carl Laemmle, Jr., and Ida Lupino; and

105

106

first timers George Raft and Virginia Hill. Pat DiCicco with Sally Blane, the Howard Greens, the Daryl Zanucks, and tons more were also there. Howard Grieves's interior received rave reviews, most commentators noting the Trocadero's suave cream-colored walls with a hint of gold in the molding, as well as the ornate chandeliers and striped silk chairs.

By all standards, Wilkerson's Trocadero was a bona fide success. By tossing this latest hat into Hollywood's nightlife ring, he virtually ushered in Hollywood's golden age of glamour. The film colony finally had its own official playground, sanctioned by the stars and their studios, and officially legal by virtue of Prohibition's repeal and the club's own no-gambling policy. The Trocadero became the focal point in town to see and be seen, the stars' idea of a perfect nightclub, a place so thick with actors and actresses that it was thought of more as someone's party den than a public nighterie. But where other clubs had failed due to their exclusivity, the Troc flourished, mixing exposure with intimacy to satisfy both publicists and stars.

Wilkerson also initiated a Sunday night audition policy, where newcomers had a chance to perform in full view of the mightiest powers in Hollywood. Sunday night soon became *the* night to head for the Troc—not only for the array of talent on display, but also because of Los Angeles's dated Blue Laws, which prohibited dancing within city limits on the Sabbath.

Above. Jimmy Stewart mugs for a fascinated
Ginger Rogers at the Troc.

Opposite. David Niven, Sally Blane, Cesar
Romero, and Sherman Rogers share a joke
at the Troc.

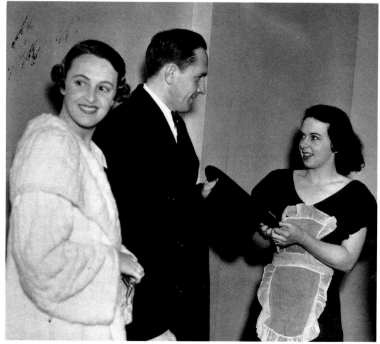

A gallery of Trocadero guests. Opposite top left. Randolph Scott, William Frawley, Leroy Prinz, Bob Burns and wife.
Top right. Maxine the check girl greets Mr. and Mrs. Frederic March.
Bottom left. Ida Lupino and Louis Hayward.
Bottom right. Cesar Romero ''races'' Douglas Fairbanks, Jr., and Betty Furness.

Above. Phil Ohman's orchestra capitalized on its Trocadero association as house band in this sheet music cover.

In the shadow of the Trocadero's enormous success, other clubs sprang up all along Sunset, making the boulevard one long procession of nocturnal merrymaking. On opening night at the Club Madrid down the street from the Troc, a couple of gents from the fighting profession initiated the club with a fistfight brought on by exchanged sarcasms. The ensuing melee alerted the local law, who broke up the fight and in the process discovered that the place was violating local liquor laws. Manager James Utley was promptly pinched. Witnessing the opening ceremonies at ringside were perennial clubbers Joan Bennett and her husband Gene Markey, Sally Blane and Allan Mowbry, who concluded the evening's festivities with an impromptu rendition of ''Wearin' O The Green,'' in an attempt to smooth things over. Also debuting about the same time as the Troc were a smattering of clubs in the hills about the boulevard.

Above the Club Ballyhoo, hidden among the eucalyptus and mesquite, Club Mont-Aire on Harold Way was one of those discreet clubs that offered a variety of entertainment, depended on little advertising, and existed largely by word of mouth. Sequestered away from the flashier spots on the Strip, but near enough to enjoy its fame, the converted hillside Spanish-style homes, plain on the outside, comfortable inside, were discreet hideaways for publicity-shy funseekers. Several doors away from the Mont-Aire, and a decade later, one of the Hollywood's premiere madames, Brenda Al-

109

110

Don the Beachcomber, a few steps off of Hollywood Boulevard, was a tropical paradise of bamboo, bananas, and Chinese cuisine.

len, conducted her business until the vice squad closed it down in 1948.

Away from the Trocadero and the Strip, nightclub action continued at a furious pace. The legendary Don the Beachcomber began serving his rum concoctions in the corner of a small hotel bar on McCadden Place shortly after the repeal of Prohibition, and the exotic blend of his tropical drinks and the South Seas decor was a winning combination in a town hungry for the novel and new. Originally the place was a bamboo bar seating twenty-five between two phony palms. Once the movie trade sampled Don's Zombies and Missionary's Downfalls, the rush was on. Don, who had his name legally changed to the Beachcomber, bolstered his success with his "rum rhapsodies," and with his future wife Sunny Sund, who took over the reins of the operation soon after Don hit paydirt. The famous Zombie was invented for a customer with an overripe hangover, who requested the master barkeeper to prepare a concoction that would alleviate his misery and see him through a business meeting in the evening. Don took one ounce each of six different rums, combined them with some secret ingredients, and poured the results in a long slender glass. The customer downed the drink and went off to his meeting. When he returned, the customer replied to Don's inquiry about the drink's effectiveness, "It made a zombie of me—I felt like the living dead." From then on, any customer requesting the specialty was lim-

111

Claudette Colbert and escort Travis Banton at a Beverly Hills affair.

112

ited to two per visit. Other original Beachcomer drinks included the Shark's Tooth, the Vicious Virgin, the Never Say Die, the Cobra's Fang, and the PiYi, served in a miniature pineapple.

The Chinese cuisine, another fresh taste for the movie crowd, kept the tiny place jumping until the bar and restaurant outgrew their quarters. Within a couple of years, the whole operation moved across the street to larger accommodations, and a velvet rope was installed for the lines waiting to get in. The building, which resembled a boxy stucco apartment, was surrounded by a thicket of bamboo, and any blatant signage announcing the location was removed, so famous had it become. Also installed in the new version was an open court with real palm trees, a Chinese grocery store just inside the door, a rum shop, a gift shop, and a lei shop. Tables were made of varnished monkey pod wood and situated in a way that gave each customer the impression of being "on an island for two." The dim interior was also calibrated so that it would be "the kind of lighting that would conceal lines in faces and make every woman look lovely and mysterious." The meandering rooms were given names such as the Black Hole of Calcutta and the Cannibal Room, and here and there were bunches of real bananas for patrons to pluck off and eat. Water was sprayed from the ceiling onto a tin roof, creating the din of a tropical rainstorm, and the flow emptied into planters behind glass partitions. Fresh flower leis were flown

Cafe Society and attentive bartenders at Club Versailles on the Strip.

in three times a week to adorn the necks of alluring stars; and for regular customers such as Joan Crawford, Dixie Lee and Bing Crosby, Rudy Vallee, and Marlene Dietrich, a special case was provided for their personal chopsticks.

As 1934 drew to a close, Hollywood was prospering. The Depression seemed to be taking a rest—in Tinseltown anyway. The public was movie-mad, and the film industry was busy satisfying its customers. Nighttime ramblings were de rigeur for anyone who had made it or was on the way up. No longer was a night on the town an optional fling. Studio publicists encouraged and even arranged for their wards to be seen at the latest club or smart party. And for those already at the top, it was good policy to let the fans and columnists get a glimpse of their favorites at play.

On the eve of Thanksgiving, cinemaland devotees got such a chance when the season opened with the Screen Actors Guild Ball at the new Biltmore Bowl. Chairman George Montgomery was assisted by Jimmy Cagney and Joe E. Brown in throwing the town's hottest bash of the year. Montgomery and Ann Harding led the Grand March, after which the crowd, including Claudette Colbert, Roland Young, Ann Sothern, Edward G. Robinson, and George Raft, danced the latest crazes—the Continental and the La Cucaracha. The same evening, Warner Brothers premiered its latest musical sensation, *Flirtation Walk*, at Warners Hollywood Theater.

113

The Vine Street Derby was an immediate focal
point of Hollywood social activity when it
opened in Hollywood in the early '30s.

Above. An early '30s view of the Hollywood
Brown Derby minus the signature caricatures
on its walls.

Right. The Derby Bar, mid '30s, with Eddie
Vitch caricatures in place.

116

Above. The Hollywood Derby's interior about 1936 with the favored left-side booths.

Left. 21 Club owner Jack Kneider mugs with friends at a Derby lunch.

Victor Hugo's at Wilshire and Beverly Drive in Beverly Hills became a local favorite for high-class parties when it moved from its downtown location in December 1934.

For Thanksgiving, many of Hollywood's elite chose Agua Caliente to spend the extended weekend, among them recently arrived Merle Oberon. New to town, Merle was being introduced to Hollywood by old acquaintance Douglas Fairbanks, whose whirlwind tour included lunch at The Vendome with Maurice Chevalier, and an evening at the Clover Club, where a party was thrown in her honor. Welcoming her were Howard Hughes and Marilyn Marsh, the Irving Berlins, the Sam Goldwyns, Harpo Marx, and Claire Windsor, who drew the spectators' applause when she joined headliners Ramon and Rosita in a rhumba.

As December rolled around, optimism and party planning seemed to pervade the whole of Southland society. The local Hearst paper, *The Examiner*, posted the year's most popular stars, starting with Will Rogers, followed by Clark Gable, Janet Gaynor, Wallace Beery, Mae West, Joan Crawford, Bing Crosby, Shirley Temple, Marie Dressler, and ending up with Norma Shearer, which set the town tongues wagging.

The Victor Hugo, long a popular first-class restaurant in downtown Los Angeles, moved to the posher Beverly Hills, opening on December 10 at 233 North Beverly Drive. Hugo Aleidas announced that festivities would begin at 11 A.M., and the film folk flocked into the place like lemmings. Beverly Hills had a new place to parade in.

In anticipation of the Christmas Holidays, United Airlines was offering jaunts,

117

Above. Jean Harlow in a glib moment at the Cocoanut Grove.

Opposite above. Jimmy Cagney dines at the Vine Street Derby with William Cagney, Boots Mallory, Phil Regan, and Josephine Dwyer.

Opposite below. The Bamboo Bar at the Hollywood Derby.

118

down to Caliente in a mere fifty-six minutes from Hollywood. The spa itself advertised accommodations at $4.50 a night during the week, with $.50 additional tariff for weekends, and that included the Dinner Dansant. With a good number of movie industry personnel earning in the five- or six-figure bracket annually, the south-of-the-border junket left plenty of dough to feed the slot machines and roulette wheels in the casino.

The gambling mania that seemed to grip the famous like a fever wasn't their vice alone. In the depths of the Depression, all America was willing to gamble what dollars they had in almost any game of chance that came along. The press reported that some thirteen million were involved weekly. Newspapers blared: "Americans are tossing their hard-earned money at the feet of the goddess of chance and taking an awful trimming." It was no wonder that gaming clubs throughout Hollywood prospered and that the law seemed to be chasing its tail. Raid after raid netted owners a few nights of inconvenience, after which business resumed as usual. Flagrant disregard for the law was compounded by the fact that gambling was a misdemeanor where most of the clubs operated, and a few well-placed dollars usually got any guilty parties off the hook. The public had almost become conditioned to lawlessness, reflected in the crime wave sweeping the nation and the recent slayings of John Dillinger and "Babyface" Nelson. The local scene never attained that level of

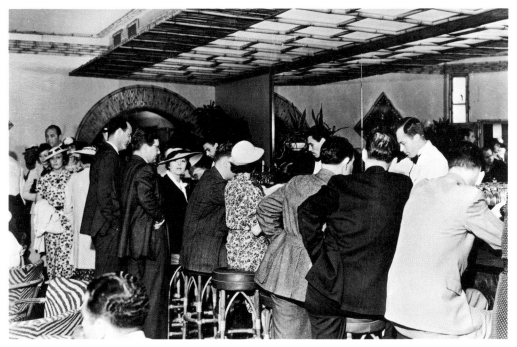

notoriety, but behind the glamour and gloss, many clubs, especially those featuring gambling, had tommy gun-toting guards to protect their investment.

In a lighter mood, all of Hollywood, it seemed, turned out for the Mayfair Ball held at the Beverly Wilshire, with W. C. Fields and George Raft heading the bill. The social crowd of Los Angeles and Hollywood was still tingling, it was reported, several days after the early December affair.

In the ever-popular Trocadero, male celebs gathered for a stag party given by movie exec Joe Schenck to congratulate Daryl Zanuck on the birth of his son Richard. Among the two dozen notables attending were Louis B. Mayer, Michael Curtiz, Wallace Beery, Sid Grauman, Frederic March, Irving Thalberg, Hal Roach, Harry Cohn, and Irving Berlin.

Also noted by the Hollywood grapevine was George Burns and Gracie Allen's nightclubbing at the Clover with Jack Haley, and, of course, Lupe and Johnny's perpetual attendance at the American Legion fights.

The big news for racing fans was the Christmas opening of the new Santa Anita racetrack in nearby Arcadia. The polo pack of Disney, Zanuck, and company had their season boxes secured, but a host of others were left in the cold with standing-room-only predicted for the season.

Citing all the obvious prosperity, headlines proclaimed Los Angeles's best Christmas season since the crash of 1929. The media decried the growing up of

119

120

Above. Stewart Erwin and June Collyer at the Beverly Wilshire's Mayfair Garden Ball.

Opposite. Perino's first location replaced Herbert Somborn's Hi-Hat Cafe on a swank stretch of Wilshire near Western.

Hollywood from village to city, as well as the tremendous output of movies, with current production schedules averaging six weeks. The enthusiasm spilled over to the celebrating film populace, who planned to enter 1935 with a bang. The Brown Derby introduced its new cocktail lounge to the holiday crowd, and offered its regulars complimentary Tom & Jerrys. The Roosevelt closed the venerable Blossom Room, remodeled it in a Persian style, with gold silk canopies and candlelight, and rechristened the dining room with a five-dollar-a-plate dinner several days before the New Year.

For New Year's eve, the barometer of the city's nightlife, celebrations ranged from the elaborate to the sublime. Tourists streamed into the city in record numbers, with a dozen extra Southern Pacific trains depositing the visitors and the hotels jammed with revelers. The enthusiastic film colony reciprocated by showing up in force. The hotels had been sold out for weeks, and crowds overflowed in the Hollywood Plaza and the Roosevelt. At the Ambassador, 1,200 guests greeted the New Year in the Cocoanut Grove, while the Little Club adjacent to the Grove was the scene of heavy celebrity activity. At the Trocadero, Louis B. Mayer entertained a table for seventy of his guests; Myron and David Selznick for twenty, and Harry Cohn for twelve. Marlene Dietrich made a grand entrance accompanied by husband Hans Sieber and Prince Felix Rolo of Egypt. On the dance floor could be spotted Clark Gable,

The Wilshire Bowl on the "Miracle Mile" treated film celebs to dining and dancing, frequently headlining popular Phil Harris. It was later reincarnated as Slapsy Maxie's.

Above. The Wilshire Bowl bar.

Howard Hughes, Colleen Moore, Gloria Swanson, Richard Barthelmess, and Harold Lloyd.

Everywhere it seemed that old man Depression was being drowned and forgotten, as throngs massed in capacity crowds. Autograph hounds stationed themselves at the Biltmore Bowl, the Palomar Ballroom, the Town House, Perino's, and Lindy's on Wilshire. Limousines slinked toward the beaches, as stars embarked on water taxis to the gambling ship *Monte Carlo*, or were deposited along the boardwalk to dance at Casino Gardens to Dick Sudbury's and Tex Howard's bands. Frank Sebastian was on hand as usual, dispensing greetings, merriment, and his traditional ham and eggs at dawn. In Glendale, at the Continental Club, which was under the auspices of Nola Hahn and the Clover Club, Cab Calloway was Hi-Dee-Ho'ing to a packed house, and, as usual, downtown Los Angeles was a madhouse, with traffic-stopping masses partying in the streets and club-hopping from the Cafe De Paree to the 41 Club to the Club LaSalle, "Where Every Night is New Year's Eve."

Post-New Year's partying was marred by yet another raid conducted by the Sheriff's Department. On the Strip, deputies closed down the Club Esquire, owned by Danny Dowling, a former dancing partner of Joan Crawford, with the typical pre-repeal raid for illegal sale of hard liquor. Dowling was nowhere to be found for questioning. Other club owners

Musso and Franks was already a tradition by the·' 30s.

Opposite. Naughty and bawdy Tijuana continued to be a filmland favorite destination throughout the '30s.

124

weren't as fortunate. Milton ''Farmer'' Page and Nola Hohn of the Clover Club were served with subpoenas, and a short-lived headline war against gambling concerns was on again. When the Lindbergh kidnapping case went to trial a few days later in New Jersey, all the hubbub over illegal gambling disappeared, and Hollywood became more concerned about Lupe filing for divorce from Johnny than the presence of harmless roulette wheels in Sunset Boulevard clubs.

In February, the perennial Frank Sebastian inaugurated his twelfth year in business at his Culver City location. Open for 4,015 consecutive nights, Frank treated his guests to a thousand-pound birthday cake presented by Tom Mix, Monte Blue, and Lyle Talbot. Les Hite was engaged for the musical portion of the celebration, and dancers ''floated'' on the West's first aerial dance floor. The revue featured a cast of fifty-six in ''The Greatest Aggregation of Creole Talent Ever Assembled in a Cafe.'' Frank knew how to throw a party, and Tinseltown never failed to show up.

That same night, back on the Strip, Hollywood's newest playhouse and nightspot bowed to the private sector of the elite. Guy Rennie's King's Club, for members only, was the brainchild of an entrepreneur who had previously owned clubs in London, New York, and Paris. Rennie worked with two partners, socialite and bon vivant Jack Beckham and Bruce Knox, interior decorator to Franchot Tone and Joan Crawford. Admit-

tance to the powder blue and white room was by gold keys issued to members, and Hollywood's newest innovation was introduced, a champagne hour, which was later than the usual cocktail hour and "swankier."

Also in February, *It Happened One Night* swept the Academy Awards, with stars Claudette Colbert and Clark Gable receiving top honors, and the fan magazines were all agog with the renaissance in nightlife. *Motion Picture Magazine* offered a tour of gastronomic hot spots, declaring that Hollywood had come of age and actors were becoming cuisine-conscious epicures. At Eddie Brandstatter's Sardi's, it was revealed that Marlene Dietrich enjoyed the chicken hamburger, which combined dark meat and pork, and was covered with melted butter. Maurice Chevalier, on the other hand, stuck to simple fare almost always accompanied by Chianti wine. Another Spartan eater was Katharine Hepburn, who usually asked for a lettuce and tomato salad, along with artichoke hearts and tongue. Wallace Beery displayed a commoner's taste for grilled cheese sandwiches, hamburgers, or ham and eggs; while Joan Crawford dined on prunes stuffed with cottage cheese.

The Russian Eagle on Vine Street was another stop on the pilgrimage. General Theodor Lodijensky presided over this establishment, among whose frequent visitors was the elusive Greta Garbo, who always sat in the far right corner as you entered. The gypsy trio and the flickering

125

126

Ever present in the '30s, gambling ships such as the Monte Carlo *plied West Coast waters catering to the movie crowd.*

candlelight seemed to suit the Silent One as she consumed a pound of the freshest Beluga caviar served by the fezzed and red-smocked waiters. More often than not, another pound of the sturgeon eggs accompanied her home. Her buying habits weren't the only reason for the owner's fondness for his premier customer. " 'Garbo is very considerate,' says Old Russia's General. 'I notice that when she is someone's guest, she always orders the dinner, table d'hôte, with no specialties. It is a flat sum, you see. But when she is alone, or the hostess, she orders anything she chooses, because she will pay the check.' " Other guests of the establishment included Lillian Harvey, who preferred a glass of vodka accompanying her shashlik, a Caucasian dish of barbecued pickled lamb. Janet Gaynor was partial, when she arrived by car, to hailing headwaiter Count Leo Tolstoi, who would then summon the General to chaperone her inside, when she was unaccompanied by an escort.

Also on the itinerary were LaGolondrina, a reconverted wine cellar on Olvera Street in downtown Los Angeles, where, among the marimba bands and petticoated señoritas, everyone from Jean Harlow and Anna May Wong to Eleanor Roosevelt and Will Rogers delighted in Mexican specialties; and, of course, an obligatory stop at the town's premiere spots, The Vendome and the Trocadero, rounded out the journey.

Not only was the town's cuisine-consciousness being raised, but it seemed

*Mr. and Mrs. Charles Winniger and Mr. and
Mrs. Joe Penner viewing the Colony Club's
entertainment.*

FLASH!

Edgar **BERGEN**

AND *Charlie* **McCARTHY**

the team that sky-rocketed to fame

with *George* **OLSEN**
AND HIS ORCHESTRA

will open **JUNE 1st** at the

Ambassador
"COCOANUT GROVE"

GALA OPENING PARTY *with Guest Stars* **TUES. EVE., JUNE 1st**

Fred MacMurray and Rhea Marion at Cafe Lamaze.

Hollywoodites were going dressy in a big way. Nighttime rambles were bringing out the best in mid-'30s stars. Gone were the days of dropping into a club in beach pajamas or a polo shirt. Instead, tails and ties were de rigeur, and milady was stepping out in chiffon and satin. Columnist Cornelius Vanderbilt, Jr., illustrated the point at the opening of Club Continental overlooking the airport in Burbank. "The most attractive salle was packed with as distinguished a crowd of luminaries as I've seen since the party at the Mayfair in December. And it is truly a gorgeous room, formal yet intime. Its sloped roof is carved and paneled and tinted in shades that give it an air of respectability as well as gayety. The orchestral pit is done in the lightest of blues with caricatured stars from the heavens vying and outshining those of Hollywood who were swaying about on the dance floor.

"I took sprightly Paulette Goddard with me. Her furs were draped in such a way about her as to project her right into the spotlight every moment of the time. Again poor Charlie had to work, or I would have felt most guilty about it. . . . Near us sat the Jack Kirklands. She is lovelier looking every time I see her. . . . Her red brocaded cape, threaded with quilted gold, had them all staring their eyes out. Jack wrote the very, very successful *Tobacco Road* and lots of other things. He is as nice a chap as you'd ever want to meet.

"Howard Hughes, all his six feet two

130

enveloped in not too exaggerated full-dress suit, looked bored except when sylphlike Marion Marsh, her head ring-leted in thousands of tiny blonde curls, was dancing in his arms. Then he would smile and hug her a bit closer. With them was Colleen Moore in yellow chiffon. And the Joe E. Browns, who never seem to miss a party, were there too: she wearing her bird-of-paradise brown velvet toque in which she is certainly most effective.

''The party wound up at six, and from then until away past nine they gathered in little clusters at Sardi's, the many Brown Derbys, and the Armstrong and Schroeders, for a 'sup-fest' (which is Hollywood's latest interpretation of the supper-breakfast combination).''

At another affair at the Troc, Vanderbilt reported: ''Thus after an unannounced preview the other evening I was agreeably surprised to find George Arliss sitting at the next table to mine at the fashionable Trocadero. I was dinner-coated, but he wore a mixed grey-blue afternoon business suit, and could have been distinguished anywhere. Nearby were the Nunnally Johnsons, and as Nunnally had done so much with Arliss I asked him how he was to work for. But Nunnally's answer was drowned out by the arrival of Clark Gable and a tiny, golden haired child with particularly large blue eyes. Bronzed, his mustache clipped close, he looked the movie-hero to perfection. . . . David Midvani, one of the Russian triplets, was nearby. It was the

131

Opposite. Phil Ohman's orchestra poses in the Trocadero cellar.

Eddie Lowe and wife leave a Trocadero fashion show.

132

Above. The American Legion Stadium behind the Hollywood Brown Derby was an entertainment staple for stars throughout the '30s.

Opposite. Ronald Reagan and starlet Susan Hayward out on their first Hollywood date.

first time I'd seen him, too, and I didn't think he looked the big, bad wolf so many have accused him of playing. Carole Lombard, an obvious beauty, was chatting with Juliette Shelby, the beauty expert, on the relative merits of different types of perfume, and I overheard Carole say in answer as to how she liked to wear hers: 'I'm greedy about it. I like to smell for blocks!' ''

By mid-year, another gambling ship joined the *Monte Carlo*, the S.S. *Tango*, also anchored off Long Beach. Gambling ace Tony Cornero, recently released from prison for bootlegging, was involved in this enterprise with manager Clarence Blazier. Tony would eventually lose his stake in the ship when a winner-take-all dice throw settled a dispute between the partners, with Tony receiving the short end of the roll. The move eventually led to Cornero's setting up his star establishment, the Rex, in a couple of years.

Summer of 1935 saw hit movies *David Copperfield* and *Anna Karenina* winning over audiences and screenland stepping into the latest place about town. In the Circus Cafe on Hollywood Boulevard, seasoned restaurateurs the Sheetz Brothers offered the film crowd an arresting underground cocktail lounge and dining room conveniently located immediately below the Screen Actors Guild offices, with direct elevator service to the room. The trick here was the circus motif done in grand style, with red and blue canvas draped along the edge of the ceiling, and cavorting small carved animals back of

133

Tony Cornero's Rex *was the most famous of the gambling brigantines.*

the bar. Palms, ivory woodwork, and a bar done in shades of cream, orange, and brown were combined to replicate, the owners were fond of saying, "a combination New York and San Francisco restaurant in the heart of Hollywood." Of course, for the stars who popped in, their privacy was closely guarded from the other customers, a maneuver accomplished by the experienced staff, whose backgrounds included positions at Texas Guinan's, the Montmartre, and the Mirador in Palm Springs. Frank Averill, manager, always attempted to give his screenland guests their desired privacy, and to keep them from becoming the objects of other customers' stares.

Along the same line, another novel attraction, the like of which was fast becoming a staple of the nightclub resurgence, was Omar's Dome on Hill Street in the heart of downtown Los Angeles, just a hop, skip, and jump from the Biltmore across Pershing Square. An alluring Persian motif was employed, with a moderne twist. Harking to the pleasure-loving philosopher Omar Khayyam, the club adopted him as spiritual godfather, decorating the walls with rich murals inspired from tales of Persian literature. Gold damask walls were trimmed in oyster white, the floor covered with a thick pile carpet of royal purple. One passed through gold mesh curtains into the main dining room, which had walls and ceiling upholstered in deep purple velvet. Circling the dance floor was a balcony covered with tufted oyster white fabric.

Robert Montgomery nibbles a carrot at Victor Hugo's.

136

*Omar's Dome was Middle Eastern exotica
served up on Hill Street in downtown Los
Angeles.*

Mr. and Mrs. George Murphy flank Roger Pryor and Ann Sothern at the Troc.

The accompanying bar, called the Oasis Room, rivaled the main salon for overdone detail. A fifty-two foot mahogany bar was faced with coral glass and strips of stainless steel. The ceiling was painted in gradations from orange through gold to ivory—all of which was lit indirectly. Orange leather stools lined the bar, and the booths were deep brown. Indeed, the whole experience was enough to make even the most jaded pub-crawler gasp.

The frequency of club openings (and closings) in the mid-'30s continued at a manic pace. The Eastern soothsayers who had dismissed the West Coast as one big provincial orange grove were taking a closer look at how much the Hollywood of yesteryear had matured into a raucous city of unlimited nightlife. Among the restaurants and clubs available at mid-decade were the Queen on Sunset, an English bar-restaurant; the Marcell Inn in Altadena, which was a favored spot for post-race fans homeward bound from Santa Anita; Frogland on Ventura Boulevard in the Valley, which featured—what else?—frog legs; and Jack Dempsey's Nite Club on Sixth at Westlake. Lindy's on Wilshire, yet another Eddie Brandstatter enterprise, featured sizzling steaks and chops at sixty-five cents a dinner. Other popular spots were the Gay Nineties on Vine Street; Jerry's Joynt in Chinatown, whose slogan "That strange place of elbowing" was made stranger by the serving of much sought-after barbecued ribs in a dining room surmounted with a gilt Buddha; the Nikabob at Ninth and

137

138

Opposite. Thelma Todd, the ''Ice Cream Blonde,'' held forth at her restaurant near Malibu until her mysterious death in her home above the club.

Above. The interior of Thelma Todd's cocktail lounge.

Western, designed in the latest moderne style; Lucy's across from Paramount Studios, done up in medieval Italian and heavily trafficked by studio employees in makeup and costume; Ollie Hammond's, another steak house in the Wilshire District that had a loyal celebrity following; the Chapeau Rouge on the Strip, and on and on and on.

Hollywood scandals, which had pretty much settled down since the '20s, broke out anew with the death of Thelma Todd a few days before Christmas 1935. Thelma, tabbed ''The Ice Cream Blonde,'' was a comedienne of some stature who was well liked in the film community. She had been married to theatrical agent and man-about-town Pat DeCicco, and was also co-owner of her own star hangout, Thelma Todd's Sidewalk Cafe, midway between Malibu and Santa Monica. The night of her death she had attended a party as guest of honor at the Tocadero, where host Stanley Lupino and his daughter Ida reported Miss Todd in lively spirits, having danced most of the night. When she left the Troc at around three in the morning, it was the last anyone saw of her. The next day her maid discovered her slumped behind the wheel of her car midway up the hill in a garage behind her cafe. A possible murder, the case was never solved, though the headlines blared forth right through the holidays with every lead and suspicion until there was nothing left to report.

By the time New Year's Eve rolled around, the film colony was hard at work

139

Lucey's across from Paramount studios on Melrose Avenue was a popular gathering spot for stars from other studios as well.

smoothing over the bad news about Thelma and looking forward to yet another Sunset Strip boite opening. Al de Freitas, a local fixture on the nightclub scene and a former assistant film director, knew just what the film folk wanted when he debuted his Club Seville on December 30. The white-faced stone building housed Hollywood's first crystal dance floor in the Crystal Marine Room. First-nighters Jean Harlow and Bill Powell, the Pat O'Briens, Robert Taylor, Glenda Farrell, Frances Langford, and others gaily danced on the see-through floor, under which fish cavorted, stimulated by variegated lights and fountains. In the Circle Room, each guest was greeted by a page, who served a complimentary cocktail. In the Arabian Room, dinner was prepared by Marcel Lamaze, the town's number one epicure.

As with the year before, 1936 was welcomed with a bigger bang than ever. The massive Palomar ballroom had recently been remodeled; cocktail lounges and soda fountains were added, without changing the exotic Arabian decor. New Year's celebrants could wheel their cars to the attendant at the Promenade entrance, settle in at a ringside table, sample a complimentary champagne cocktail, enjoy a full course dinner while being entertained by the Hudson–Metzger dancing girls, dance to Joe Venuti's music, and cheer the New Year in with the hats and noisemakers provided at each table for the fifty-dollar tab.

The oddball event of the season was

140

produced by scenarist Al Martin, who took over the Lido Room of the Knickerbocker Hotel for a pooch party, inviting the canine pals of Joan Crawford, Stu Erwin, Ruth Collier, Mervyn LeRoy, and assorted others. Their owners were invited also, but only if the chaperones wore evening clothes. In the event some of the pets got into a scrap over each other's food, two ambulances were on hand to administer emergency service.

Impromptu entertainment offered by some of the stars never failed to extract unbounded enthusiasm from fans and fellow stars alike. Bing Crosby and wife Dixie Lee treated an audience at the Century Club on Beverly Boulevard one Sunday night, when Bing took the stage and belted out ''Dinah'' and ''I Kiss Your Lucky Hand, Madame,'' and Dixie sang ''Lucky Star'' to a crowd that included Joe Venuti and Zeppo Marx. Joining the festivities was Jimmy Dorsey, performing a cornet solo, and the evening ended with Bing joining master of ceremonies Billy Gray and Jerry Bergen in a comedy routine.

Hollywood in 1936 was a town fulfilled. The national economy was recovering, and moviemaking and moviegoing were national pastimes. All eyes were on Hollywood, not only as an escape for the less fortunate around the country, but also because the business of glamour was a worldwide fixation. It seemed everyone followed the stars' lives, from the most intimate to the most mundane of details. High on the list, of

141

The Zenda Ballroom drew stars to the downtown area of 7th Street and Figueroa.

Opposite. An orchestra awaits the crowds of the Tango Club at a spacious Zenda Ballroom.

142

course, was what movie folk did when they were not before the camera. The fan magazines, in their incessant scrutiny of notables, provided a somewhat accurate picture, if sometimes through rose-tinted glasses. *Screen Guide*, in a 1936 issue, took its readers on a heady spree through Hollywood at night, led by writer Kay Proctor and escort Cesar Romero. The premise of the tour was to give all those ''nice kids'' across the country an idea of what a one-night fling would do to their pocketbooks if they could manage to land in Tinseltown for at least one night.

The memorable evening commenced at seven in the Bamboo Room of the Hollywood Brown Derby. As Miss Proctor described it: ''It is a fairly large room with low tables and chairs, for a change, instead of spacious booths which seem so prevalent this year. It takes its name obviously from the wall paneling of split bamboo. . . . Bob Cobb is the genial host and the ordinary drinks—cocktails, fizzes, highballs, etc.—average 30 cents a copy. If your taster wants teasing, I recommend the house specialty, a Bamboo. It's fashioned from Bacardi and limes and costs 40 cents. . . . Before we left we said hello to George Raft, who was going someplace in a hurry; Pat and Eloise O'Brien; Marie 'Dumb-pan' Wilson and her beau, Director Nick Grinde; Fred MacMurray and Lillian back from their Hawaiian honeymoon and young Tom Brown, apparently cast as a lone wolf for the evening.'' For dinner, Cesar chose

144

Opposite. A remodeled King's Tropical Inn in Culver City continued to pack 'em in throughout the '30s.

Above. Rudy Vallee headlined at the Grove in 1938 while an amorous Cesar Romeo gives Emily Dean a peck on the cheek at the Tropics.

the Cocoanut Grove and a meal which set the twosome back $14.50 for couvert, appetizer, soup, filet mignon, wine, tax, and tip. Included in the price was a dance floor where they rubbed shoulders with Bette Davis and bandleader–husband Harmon Nelson; Ginger Rogers with Johnny Green; Claudette Colbert and husband Joel Pressman; Joan Blondell and Dick Powell; and Robert and Betty Young. For liqueurs, the next stop was up to the Strip at Danny Dowling's Club Esquire, followed by the mandatory visit to the Trocadero, ''the most famous—and costly—of Hollywood's night spots.'' Again, Kay explains: ''The Troc is divided into two parts, the street floor, or cafe proper, and the Cellar. Swank hold forth upstairs, good fellowship down. . . . Upstairs decorations feature plain cream walls with a touch of gold in the moldings and beautiful light fixtures. The Cellar, in keeping with its spirit, has walls paneled in stained oak and wooden ceiling with the graining set in oblique pattern. The bar itself is of gleaming, highly polished copper. Ask for 'Tex'. . . . Drinks run from 60 cents to $1.50. That one-fifty number, in case you are interested, is a lulu called 'French 75' or 'T.N.T.' By way of warning, it is just that—dynamite. . . . Another daisy is the 'Vendome Special Sling' ($1.00) in which the bartender makes magic out of ginger beer, cherry brandy, gin and lime juice. The house special is the 'Trocadero Cooler' for 75 cents, a tall, frosted concoction.''

145

146

Sharing a table at the Troc in 1936 are
director Wesley Ruggles and Fred MacMurray
and their companions.

Opposite. The Ambassador Hotel's Cocoanut
Grove still held forth as Hollywood's premier
'30s gathering spot.

Since the couple was only stopping
for drinks, they didn't venture upstairs
but headed for the Cellar where, sipping
their scotch-and-sodas, they exchanged
pleasantries with James Stewart and Betty
Furness, Clark Gable and Carole Lombard, and Bill Powell and Jean Harlow.
Upon exiting they ran into Myrna Loy
and husband, Gene Raymond and Jeanette
MacDonald, Joan Crawford and hubby
Franchot Tone, Bob and Betty Montgomery, and studio mogul L. B. Mayer.
From there, it was on to the Casanova
Club, "a stone's throw from the Troc,"
where the decor was accentuated by a
dark blue canopy covering the ceiling
and murals reproducing street scenes from
Paris's Latin Quarter. There the featured
drink was the "Casanova Cocktail," vio-
let in color and packing a punch. The
final stop for the evening was the Melody Grill, the "hot spot" of Sunset. For
nightcaps, Kay and Cesar could choose
from the "Moist Rhapsody" and the
"Passion Ball" or the "Crooner's Alibi"
and the "Composer's Revenge." They
wisely stuck to their scotch-and-sodas
while listening to the dusky songs of Cleo
Brown. Although Cesar suggested scram-
bled eggs at all-night Sardi's, Kay elected
to go home for a well-deserved rest. Com-
puting the tabs the next morning, the
author reported the financial damage at a
modest $21.55 for their evening of fun.
As a postscript to those who actually
might manage the pilgrimage, Miss Proctor advised them to have their own car,
because taxis were generally unavailable;

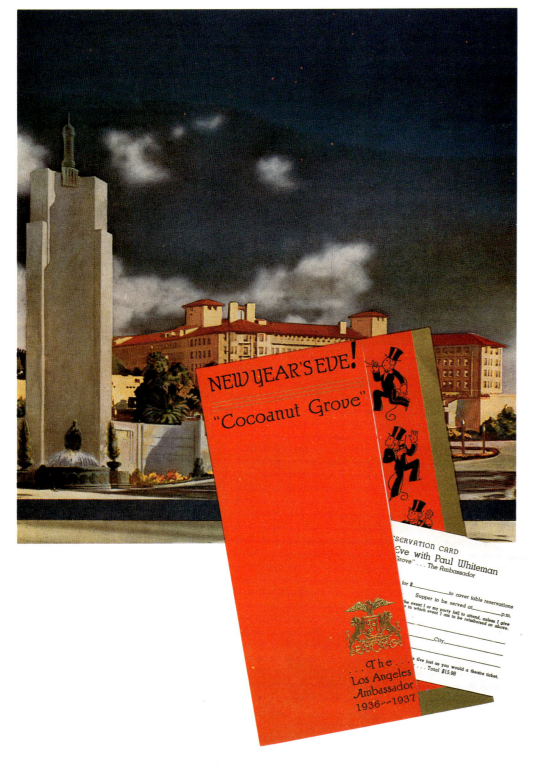

to dress as well as possible, because of the fierce competition; and above all, not to stare at the stars, who were technically not on public display!

In the Hollywood of 1936, Tuesdays at the Grove were still immensely popular. The passing years had only embellished the nightspot's reputation, which included in its annals a fair share of fights and romances. One memorable battle, dubbed ''The War of the Red Noses,'' involved Ruby Keeler and husband Al Jolson, who, verbally assaulted by a group of drunks, proceeded to slam the offenders across the dance floor, starting instantaneous pandemonium among the Grove's patrons and staff. Bandleader Abe Lyman rushed from the rest room and gathered his band from intermission to strike up a brisk fox-trot as diversion, but to no avail. By the time the screams had subsided, the Grove was a shambles.

Of course Lupe and Johnny stirred up a few scrapes at the Grove, as they did almost everywhere they went. Lupe explained the scuffles: ''Johnny take me to the Grove every week, and do we dance? No! He go to hear gossip. He say: 'Lupe, go to the lounge and see what's new.' If I come back with no new gossip, bingo! And when we fight, we t'row t'ings!''

Adding to the Grove's glamour were the Academy Awards, which had taken place there since 1930. But 1936 was the last year the Grove played host, and it was also the last year a banquet was presented in conjunction with the event. The hotel nonetheless continued to ac-

147

Interior of the Cocoanut Grove in 1936.

commodate the needs of the stars, and opened the Ambassador Lounge adjacent to the Cocoanut Grove, and the Fiesta Room, decorated in gold and cerulean, its entrance surmounted by a statue of Bacchus. For the overflow crowds, it became a cozy rendezvous, and it was often taken over for private parties.

Over at another Hollywood hostelry, the Roosevelt, a similar setup had been initiated the previous fall and dubbed the Cine-Grill. Its interior boasted, behind the bar, a mural of vintage moving pictures, though the room itself was decidedly in the modern mode. A typically Hollywood premiere opening pulled the film folk in, and it became an alternate post from which to sip exotic cocktails and go over the daily rounds of gossip. In contrast to other establishments that seemed to reach into past decades for inspiration, the Cine-Grill went full-tilt into the future. Deep red Formica, then a new material, covered the bar front, which was trimmed with horizontal chrome stripes and lit indirectly from beneath the mahogany top. The stools along the bar were designed to resemble champagne glasses, and were covered in blue gazelle leather. In the grill, ladies could peer from their chrome tube chairs at the passing parade through mirrored Venetian blinds flanked by beige draperies trimmed with maroon rope swags.

Not to be outdone by its neighboring hotel, and certainly realizing a market to exploit, the Hollywood Plaza on Vine threw its hat into the ring and opened the

149

Two visitors in the Cinnabar relax in 1936 luxury.

150

Cinnabar in December of 1936. Ads proclaimed it "So Breathtaking in its Beauty . . . So Different in its Conception . . . It will Live Forever in the Romantic Pages of Hollywood History!" For ten dollars first-nighters could partake of "history in the making," and be serenaded by Anne Crosby and the Four Avalon Boys, sip champagne, and be coddled by maitre d'hotel Albert, Hollywood's favorite greeter, who remembered the favorite dish of nearly every Hollywood celebrity. The $125,000 room drew a slate of notables to the opening-night fest, with manager Tom Hull throwing the switch to unveil the mural of filmland life, similar to the Cine-Grill's, and christening the writers' and directors' corners. Also planned was a replica of a street in old Mexico adjacent to the restaurant, rambling through an outdoor palm grove dotted with barbecue pits, strolling caballeros, and dancing señoritas.

Drifting toward Beverly Hills, another gentleman, transplanted from New York, was also thinking about barbecue pits. Dave Chasen, a vaudevillian and partner with one Joe Cook, found himself at the end of his career by the mid-'30s. Harold Ross, editor of *The New Yorker* and a mutual friend of the duo, agreed to advance Chasen $3,000 to open a restaurant in Hollywood, based only on his memory of Chasen's expertise in the kitchen—the terrific meals he had prepared for weekend guests—and on blind faith that the enterprise would work.

So on December 13, 1936, Chasen

Adjoining the Hollywood Plaza Hotel is the entrance to the Cinnabar Restaurant.

opened his Southern Pit Barbecue on Beverly Boulevard near Doheny. The square stucco building contained six tables, an eight-stool counter, and a six-stool bar, and dispensed chili at twenty-five cents a bowl and a couple of barbe-cued ribs for thirty-five cents. Bar drinks were also thirty-five cents, and when word got out about the place, East Coast expatriates swarmed over the premises. Regulars who could always be found supping and dining included W. C. Fields, Nunnally Johnson, Frank Capra, Buddy Ebsen, Gene Fowler, Jimmy Cagney, and Pat O'Brien. Within a year, prodded by Ross's constant heckling and memos, the Southern Pit evolved from chili parlor to full-fledged restaurant, and, with Chasen at the helm, assumed a first-class niche in the Hollywood community. The menu was expanded to include thirty-five items, the waiters were in black and white, and the staff went from its initial three to a small army. A room was added, and a couple dozen tables set up. The place wasn't glamorous, but the clubby atmo-sphere inclined patrons to settle in for the evening as though in one big family room. With a formidable stable of big names as regulars, their antics gained mythical proportions. For a party cele-brating Jimmy Stewart's entry into matri-mony, Chasen hired a valet to feed the star, wipe his chin, and escort him to the john. For the main course, two midg-ets dressed in diapers were served on a silver platter. On another occasion, Bob Hope rode a horse through the restaurant,

151

Harry Sugarman's Tropics delighted celebrities in Beverly Hills when he opened his restaurant on Rodeo Drive in 1936.

and an inebriated Charlie Butterworth drove a Fiat into the place. Shirley Temple, accompanied by her parents, who were sipping old fashioneds, began to cry uncontrollably. When asked about her tears, she responded that she wanted a drink just like theirs. So, the bartender concocted a drink of grenadine, ginger ale, and a little fruit, presented it to the moppet, and tagged the cocktail after its first customer. In later years, Chasen's again expanded, adding a sauna and barber in the rear of the place, where the likes of Errol Flynn, Bing Crosby, and Bogart would drop in for steak, steam, and haircut. A pregnant Dorothy Lamour stated she was uncomfortable at table twelve, so Chasen had a portion of it cut out to comfortably accommodate her.

The Southern Pit Barbecue gradually became known simply as Chasen's, and the stories evolved into legends filmites loved to circulate among themselves. Hollywood now had a swanky hangout that rivaled even New York's 21 and Chicago's Pump Room. On the night Chasen's opened, the conversation certainly included news of King Edward's formal abdication of the British throne for love of Wallis Simpson. This romantic denouement stirred considerable interest among the large British filmmaking contingent in town. Other Europeans were also making a stir on the streets and sets of Hollywood. Ingrid Bergman made her first American film appearance in *Intermezzo*, which premiered just before the Christmas holidays. No doubt some of

her social time was spent at another of Hollywood's continental cafes, which also opened that fall to the delight of filmdom's gourmands.

Bit of Sweden, housed in a quaint building on the Strip, introduced Swedish-style smorgasbord to hungry actors, actresses, and agents who did business in the area. Akavit sloshed down with beer could be enjoyed on the veranda, and, on the inside, dainty cuts of ham, beef, and tongue were served by "flickas"— waitresses decked out in gingham dresses and winged lace caps. Of course, it caught the fancy of everyone on the prowl for the newest innovation, and chef Ken Hansen was soon accepting accolades that were heaped on the favored caterers to celeb appetites.

As the New Year approached, many of the city's prominent personalities were looking at the bright prospects of the film industry and reflecting on the industry's losses, including the death of Irving Thalberg. At least forty musicals were slated for or in production as 1937 approached. Technicolor was making swift inroads as a replacement for standard black-and-white, and David Selznik had just completed *A Star Is Born*. Many screen notables headed for the hinterlands for the holidays, but plenty stuck around town for year-end festivities that were heightened by some new nighttime arrivals on the club scene.

Up near Vine, which was boasting a mini-strip of its own, with clubs seemingly bottlenecked together, Spider Kelly's opened on December 10 and lured stars with its promise of being "the most unusual place in the west." *Variety* voted the Clover Club as having the "swankiest" turnout, with L. B. Mayer, Harry Cohn, Howard Strickling, Bruce Cabot, Hal Wallis, and Alfred Vanderbilt ringing in the new. Cesar Romero hosted a party for his pals at Harry Sugarman's Tropics in Beverly Hills. Ted Snyder's, another new joint on the Strip, had a goodly share of the holiday crowd when it opened on December 21st. Snyder, a songwriter, got the place going with seed money from producer Preston Sturges, who kept an irregular hand in the operations in the converted house at Sunset and Horn Avenue. That holiday season was probably its best, since the anticipated crowds never materialized afterward, and the club eventually closed two years later. Still, it served as Sturges's inspiration for his own restaurant a few years later.

Also on Vine, Hollywood's Famous Door, its entrance scribbled with countless stars' autographs, endured long lines and bustling crowds listening to the likes of Louis Prima, who had recently opened there.

The first few months of the year had evening clothes flying in and out of star closets for a whole slew of formal events that ranged from the tribute to Adolph Zukor to the premiere of *The Garden of Allah* and from the formal opening of Victor Hugo's Garden Room to All Star nights at the Cocoanut Grove and Mickey Rooney's swing orchestra playing for the

153

The Bit of Sweden on Sunset near Doheny introduced the smorgasbord in the fall of 1936 to filmites hungry for the new and novel.

154

Ben Bernie's appearance at the Grove assured sellout crowds overflowing with the cream of Hollywood's crop.

opening of a downtown supermarket.

Certainly the Zukor tribute on January 7 and Ben Bernie's opening at the Cocoanut Grove on January 15 were barometers of the times and the extent to which stars participated in the night scene. For sheer numbers, the Cocoanut Grove should have received a prize. That evening saw the following stars dancing back-to-back in the mind-boggling array of talent: Fred Astaire, Al Jolson, Eddie Cantor, Ginger Rogers, Jack Benny, Dick Powell, Betty Furness, Joan Blondell, George Raft, Alice Faye, Ruby Keeler, Ann Shirley, Cary Grant, Joe Schenck, Frank Capra, Jerome Kern, Jack Haley, Fred Waring, George Murphy, and Daryl Zanuck.

Swing bands were the rage, adulated only slightly less than the stars themselves. La Monica ballroom on the Santa Monica Pier was booking Earl Hines, Ben Pollack, and Jimmy Dorsey in 1937. The Bon-Ton, later to become Lick Pier, held its own in bookings, while old standbys such as Sebastian's Cotton Club and the various hotel rooms like the Grove and the Biltmore Bowl drew the top names that made it to the West Coast. The Avalon Ballroom in nearby Catalina was a must for the top bands, and the Club Alabam and the Plantation on Central Avenue in L.A.'s version of Harlem hopped to the heppest of the swinging tunes. But the Palomar at Vermont and Third, formerly the Rainbow Garden, was the town's premier hall for Swing after it changed hands.

6904 Hollywood Boulevard
Hollywood 28, California, U. S. A.
Opposite Grauman's Chinese Theatre

The Palomar had always been an attractive spot to drop in on, especially for the gals in Hollywood who seemed to fall for the band guys. Nearly a block long, its immense size and popular prices (forty cents for ladies, sixty-eight cents for gentlemen on weekdays), good for the floor show and Palomar Terrace restaurant, made it attractive to the big spender and five-and-dime clerk alike. What cemented the Palomar's fame, though, was the late summer evening performance of 1935 that skyrocketed Benny Goodman to fame. Goodman's tour, up until his Palomar appearance, had plodded along to half-baked responses until opening night of what was to be a month-long engagement. In the first hour, Goodman played his safe and soft tunes, but when it became apparent that the large crowd was reacting in the same way the rest of his audiences had, he began the second set with a spirited Fletcher Henderson arrangement, and the crowd went wild. The rest of his stay, extended another month, broke all existing attendance records for any place in the Los Angeles area. Goodman became the "King of Swing," and the Palomar was packed with such regulars as Barbara Stanwyck, Betty Grable, Robert Taylor, Bette Davis, and Martha Raye night after night. When the urge hit him, Jackie Cooper sat in on drums with various bands, and Jack Benny played an entire evening with Phil Harris's band. Inside the Palomar were staged such special events as the Hollywood Motion Picture Ball and the annual music jamborees,

155

Above. Bob Brooks's Seven Seas restaurant on Hollywood Boulevard featured "Rain on the Roof," native floor shows, and rum drinks that quenched "the locals'" thirst for anything tropical.

Left. Gene Krupa headlined the Palomar, Hollywood's grand dance spot of the '30s.

156

in which as many as twenty-six famous dance orchestras would take their turn on the bandstand.

Along with Big Bands, the Southland experienced what was described as the great "avalanche of bamboo" in the form of Hawaiian theme restaurants. The South Seas theme had already been put to use at Don the Beachcomber's, but the exotic spell really took off when the mainland-to-Honolulu route became fashionable with the Hollywood set, who both vacationed there and at times used the island paradise for location filming. Hawaii also played host to American servicemen, and as a strategic Pacific position was given a great deal of attention. It seemed only natural, with all the fakery abounding in Hollywood, that if you couldn't hop a ship halfway across the Pacific you could at least jump into your roadster and cruise down Melrose Avenue or Hollywood Boulevard to sample the South Seas creation of some set designer.

The Vernon Country Club, in the 1910s, had introduced a Hawaiian theme room with much success, and in 1934, Harry Sugarman, theater operator and managing director of Grauman's Egyptian Theater, had opened his Tropics on Rodeo Drive in the heart of Beverly Hills on Thanksgiving Day. His place became a fixture for many years, with ardent fans Alice Faye and the Ritz Brothers endorsing it as their favorite. King's Tropical Inn in Culver City dropped its '20s jungle look and committed the interior to serious Polynesian by the mid-'30s; and

Opposite above. Zamboanga Joe's colorful atmosphere and "Tailless Monkey" rum concoction drew more adventurous celebs to his nightclub on Slauson Avenue.

Opposite below. Host Harry "Sugie" Sugarman capitalized on the late '30s Hawaiian craze by naming cocktails on his menu after his celeb-studded clientele.

Ken's Hula Hut on Beverly Boulevard was undeniably Hawaiian. Marti's Club Hawaii took over the former site of Club Ugene at the western terminus of the Strip; spotted at its opening, meandering through the Paradise Room, the Garden Lounge, and the Jasmine Patio, were Carole Lombard, Humphrey Bogart, Bruce Cabot, and Madeline Carroll. On the outskirts of town, Luana, the "Famous Hawaiian Dancer," threw open the doors to a club named after her in Culver City, opposite the Rollerdrome; and on Slauson Avenue south of town, a gent by the name of Joe Chastek created a drink by the name of the "Tailless Monkey" and made a home for it at his club, Zamboanga, "The Most Beautiful Polynesian Paradise in the United States."

Hawaiian Bob Brooks entered his Seven Seas on Hollywood Boulevard into the sweepstakes with rain-on-the-roof and the obligatory rum concoctions; and Rena Borzage, wife of Frank, the film director, did her bit and opened the Hawaiian Paradise at 7566 Melrose in April 1936. In attempting to add interest to a well-worn theme, Mrs. Borzage decked her club with thickets of fireproof bamboo, throughout which were concealed live parrots and waving palms. The main dance floor was surrounded by a pond laden with tropical fish, and the bandstand was flanked by two cascading waterfalls emptying into the pond—which, incidentally, included a miniature model of Oahu itself. The adjoining Lanai Room had a removable roof for summer, and a glass roof for the cool months, so that when it rained, the patrons experienced the "unique sensation of dancing in a downpour without getting wet." All the South Seas places featured a form of Cantonese cuisine, and for the finicky star a good hunk of meat was always available for charcoal broiling.

About the time the Hindenburg blew up in May 1937, Hollywoodites were busy with another fad: rollerskating. The Rollerdrome in Culver City seemed a cinema favorite, no doubt because of its proximity to the studios, and the vast soundstage-size rink was the site of a multitude of private nighttime shindigs.

Disaster seemed to be in the air in 1937, and the Hollywood community, already somewhat shaken by Irving Thalberg's unexpected death the previous year, got another blow when Jean Harlow died on June 7. Hollywood nightlife lost a great reveler, and it wasn't until September that the late-nighters got back on their feet at the opening of "old timer" Clara Bow's bid into the Hollywood night scene. The "It" Club, managed by Clara and husband Rex Bell, moved into quarters occupied by the Cinnabar at the Plaza Hotel near Hollywood and Vine. Columnists remarked that Clara looked slimmer and as glamorous as ever in her splashy flowered print dress, worn for the club's opening. The business venture was to keep Clara, somewhat retired from the movie biz, occupied while husband Rex continued his career in the industry. Clara lost interest in the club after the birth of

157

160

The "It Club" featured a zodiac motif and a bar frequented by droves of Clara's old chums.

Clara Bow's "It Club" at the Hollywood Plaza Hotel bowed to the public on September 9, 1937, adding to the glamour of the intersection of Hollywood and Vine.

her second son the following year, and the "It" Club went along its merry way minus Clara's name.

In the annual tour of Hollywood for their readers, the fan magazines gave tips on where a visitor to the land-of-make-believe was most likely to spot his or her favorite. In late 1937, all the old stand-bys were mentioned: the Cocoanut Grove, the Derbys, the Troc, Al Levy's across from the Derby on Vine, and a couple of new clubs as well. Cafe Lamaze ranked high for those yearning for a first-class meal; and, for the night owl prowling the streets after the 2 A.M. curfew, the Swing Club on Las Palmas, owned by "B.B.B.," could be counted on for entertainment until the sun rose, though the reader was cautioned that even in the wee hours of the morning the lines could be ten deep, and an occasional raid was to be taken in stride, for "the patrons are never molested."

Closing out the year was the newly remodeled Trocadero's Big Apple Barn Dance, for which the Troc's favorite guests were urged to come dressed as cowboys, farmhands, country maidens, or city slickers dressed for a dude ranch. Heeding the call were Betty Grable and Jackie Coogan, Edgar Bergen, Wendy Barry, Milton Berle, Anne Shirley, John Payne, and Lana Turner, who did the "Big Apple" and "Suzy Q" until they all collapsed on the floor at the 2 A.M. closing. A similar success was the Troc's Bal Cap d'Antibes, held earlier that month, in which owner Wilkerson trans-

162

Above. Crowds jam the popular Zebra Room
at the Town House Hotel on Wilshire
Boulevard.

Left. Inside the Zebra Room patrons lounged
and danced in a smart atmosphere of
frolicking zebras and jolly simians.

formed the interior of the club into the Riviera. The costume trick here was to wear sun togs in the middle of Southern California's wet winter, and obliging star Marlene Dietrich complied, wearing her signature pants in blue; Lana Turner came in orange sweater and blue shorts; and Cary Grant modeled his outfit while squiring Phyllis Brooks. Other ringsiders adapting to the Troc's palm-decked atmosphere included Jack Oakie, leading the "Big Apple," Kay Francis, Gene Markey, Ann (10¢) Kresge, and the Countess di Frasso. For the 350 who attended, the cost of the party was tabulated at just under $5,000, and that paid for fifty-two lobsters, fifty chickens, and over one hundred pounds of meat.

As the film colony bid goodby to another year, Los Angeles politics was about to do a turnabout that would indirectly affect the state of nightlife on a permanent basis. For the better part of the decade, what could only be described as one of the most corrupt administrations in the history of the city had pretty much run things their way—which included the practice of payoffs for favors done. For a club to run smoothly, or even offer a little gambling on the sly, it was expected that the owner would visit the powers-that-be in city hall or police headquarters to avoid the possibility of pre-planned raids and general harassment. All that was about to end when in January 1938 a private investigator, one Harry Raymond, was blown up in his car while doing some snoop work into city corrup-

tion for an unpaid city hall creditor. When it was discovered that a police lieutenant close to the mayor's office was responsible for the murder, reformers who had been waiting for such a break ignited a storm of protest that eventually led to the recall of the mayor and the end of the payoff system.

The bogus raids that had been launched from time to time to appease religious groups and do-gooders suddenly changed character, and no amount of money could keep the heat off. The gangland element that kept such places as the Clover, Century, and Colony clubs afloat was slowly being flushed out of town and out of state, there to retrench. Nearby Palm Springs let it be known that gambling in their desert resort wasn't welcome either, and when the Dunes and 159 Club also closed up shop, games operators scurried even further into the mesquite to a nondescript town in Nevada called Las Vegas. The move was slow, and it would take a decade before state authorities were convinced to legalize gambling, but eventually the rise of Las Vegas would change the nature of nightlife as it was enjoyed in Hollywood in 1938.

Another hotel in the Wilshire district, just west of downtown, The Town House, joined the other big name establishments in opening a club of its own on the premises. The Zebra Room opened directly off Wilshire, and, as its name implied, the zebra theme ran throughout the swank cocktail retreat. A galloping neon zebra greeted guests, who wiped

163

164

their feet on a zebra striped mat and plunged into a room of brown and black zebra striped chairs. The square tables floating around the room were trimmed in zebra wood, as were portions of the wall. Murals showing prancing giraffes, zebras, and cocktail-sipping simians lined booths surrounding the dance floor, and a zebra wood piano was backed against coral walls and pillars of frosted glass. It was no wonder the social set was soon camped in, sipping rose-colored cocktails before heading to the Biltmore Bowl or the Cocoanut Grove for some serious dancing.

The Hawaiian craze that swept 1937 was losing steam when the rhumba bounced merrily into town and had everyone dancing to a Latin beat. Not that the La Cucaracha hadn't prepared dancers for south-of-the-border rhythms, but this new all-out assault netted a special party at the Troc, and a dance contest with winners Marlene Dietrich and Douglas Fairbanks, Jr., sharing the honors with Joe Schenck and Virginia Zanuck, Rudy Vallee and Dorothy Lamour, and Doug Fairbanks, Sr., with Lady Sylvia.

It seemed only natural for Hollywood to have a club of its own devoted to the latest dance sensation, and the La Conga was born on February 21 at 1551 Vine, between Sunset and Hollywood boulevards. First-nighters entering the club were greeted by Chiquita, a talking marionette, and escorted through arches to a patio reminiscent of a Cuban village. In the main dining room, intimate booths,

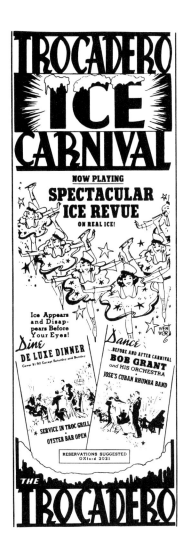

each resembling a miniature patio with tile roof and languorous palms, hovered around the dance floor, the terminus of which was a revolving bandstand that provided dancers with continuous music. Alternating between Lou Bring and his orchestra, straight from the French Casino in New York, and Eduard Duranda, featuring Chiquita, those not versed in the intricacies of the new dance could obtain free lessons from the instructors on hand. The somewhat West Indian cuisine was supplemented by the usual tariff and oriental dishes thrown in for no apparent reason. Hollywoodites made the most of the new cafe, and swarmed there en masse. Sighted in its first few months were Joan Blondell and Dick Powell, Alfred Vanderbilt, Buck Jones and spouse, and Martha Raye, with mom and step-pop in tow.

Across the street and around the corner from La Conga, the importance of the radio industry in Hollywood manifested itself in two new structures that dominated the intersection of Sunset and Vine. Both NBC, at the intersection, and CBS, east of Vine on Sunset, opened up landmark buildings as West Coast flagships for their broadcasting empires in 1938. The addition of the studios made the stretch between Sunset and Hollywood boulevards a beehive of activity. Within the two blocks were crammed Sardi's, the Coco Tree Cafe, the Brown Derby, the ''It'' Club, Mike Lyman's, La Conga, the American Legion Stadium, a couple of drive-in restaurants, the Holly-

wood Plaza Hotel, and a sprinkling of agents' offices. In the planning stage was the centerpiece of the area: Broadway producer Earl Carroll's entertainment complex on Sunset.

Billy Wilkerson, whose *Hollywood Reporter* offices were just west of the new entertainment area, pulled out stakes from the Trocadero that spring, and the Troc began to lose the dominance it had held on the Strip virtually since opening. Despite a facelift and new management, its reopening on May 18 failed to rekindle the Wilkerson touch, and the next few years saw the Troc change hands regularly. Wilkerson, however, recognizing the dramatic rise of nightlife since he opened the Troc, aggressively sought out advertisers for his tabloid and increased coverage of the night scene that same year. Not assigning himself a back seat, Wilkerson would, in a few years, open another enterprise on the Strip that would duplicate his success at the Troc.

The month of May brought the wrath of the new L.A. reformers to the club scene, as a spate of raids, this time serious, began, shaking the foundations of the formerly invulnerable gambling joints. But out on the ocean, it was another story. The S.S. *Tango*, which had languished outside Long Beach since the mid-1930s, had recently been joined by the *Caliente*, and both ships had more or less existed without inordinate harassment. But on May 5, an ex-con named Tony Cornero changed all that when he blatantly opened what is generally considered to have been

165

Opposite above. Cafe Lamaze, a swank nightspot on the Strip fed stars elegantly while La Conga on Vine Street had celebs dancing through its portals to a Latin beat.

166

Opposite. The king of the three-mile limit, the Rex was the most notable of the crafts that offered gambling to Hollywood's elite. Anchored off the Santa Monica pier in 1938, it was a constant source of irritation for lawmen who eventually closed it down.

Above. Local law enforcers making sure games of chance won't be played on the high seas.

the grandest of all the floating casinos, the *Rex*, three miles off Santa Monica Bay. Cornero, whose real name was Anthony Stralla, had consistently been involved in the gambling scene, and had served time for liquor violations during Prohibition. Back on the streets, he joined forces with the *Tango* crew, but in time grew disgruntled with the way things were being handled, and started looking around for a ship of his own. What Tony turned up was a fishing barge that he transformed with $250,000 into an arklike freighter that hardly matched the sleek ocean liner pictured in his ads. But underneath the unglamorous facade were three hundred slot machines, a bingo parlor seating five hundred, six roulette wheels, six chuck-a-luck cages, eight dice tables, keno, a faro bank, and setups for off-track betting. The main salon was 250 feet long by 40 feet wide, and featured wood paneling and several bars. The ship was also outfitted with 1,600 lifeboats, if for nothing else than to calm the nerves of customers who had read too many times about fires and sinkings of former barkentines.

Cornero blared the *Rex*'s first day of operation with full-page ads in the newspapers and airplanes flying all over Los Angeles spelling out the word "Rex" in the skies. The ads promised twenty-four-hour action, the cuisine of Henri, formerly of the Trocadero and Victor Hugo's, and dancing to the Rex Mariners—all only ten minutes from Hollywood. On the pier, a red "X" gave notice of the

boarding area, where thirteen water taxis carried customers, for twenty-five cents, on a "comfortable twelve minute ride to the *Rex*."

Tony's advertising flair paid off, according to an ad he took out a month later, which claimed the *Rex* had hosted over a million people "without injury or untoward act." Constantly salving his customers' insecurities, which were no doubt bolstered by local politicians and law enforcers' accusations, the *Rex*'s ads assured female guests, escorted or not, that they would be treated with "unfailing courtesy and rigidly enforced standards." For those concerned about their health while on board, a physician was on constant duty. All employees were stated to be American citizens registered with the Department of Commerce.

Hollywood high rollers, among them Universal head Carl Laemmle, took to the sea like seals and dropped their bucks into Cornero's coffers. The richly clad stars who were losing their gambling spots on land found the *Rex* a terrific alternative as a place to lose their shirts. For a couple of years, the *Rex* could be counted on to fill the gambling void, at least until authorities forced the ship out of business just before the war.

The night scene for the bulk of the year remained consistently active. Sidney Skolsky, columnist, reported sighting on one summer evening: Tyrone Power and Janet Gaynor dining at the Derby and being applauded by nearby diners; Paulette Goddard and the Earl of Warwick

167

sitting at the Tropics and speaking nary a word; and Bing asking Dave Chasen to turn off the radio in his restaurant because the tunes coming over the airwaves were Crosby songs. On the strip, at Ray Heller's old 9015 address, Frank Irwin opened a rather odd spot. The Mermaid Club, where bar customers could ogle a live nude ''Girl in a Fishbowl,'' used a reducing lens through which a model behind the bar seemed to be floating in an aquarium. A hop, skip, and jump eastward, Selznick's Club Versailles, resting on the slope of Sunset, faced the incredible view that seemed the ideal of every club in Hollywood. Nearby at the Troc, bubble gal Sally Rand emceed a show of her own, fully-clothed, to a sellout crowd. A few more blocks down, the Clover Club resumed booking big name draws for entertainment, and Charlie Farrell drew quite a throng for his performance, which was witnessed by Irene Dunne and Sid Grauman, among others. In Hollywood proper, Martha Raye threw a cast party for the completion of *Give Me a Sailor* at La Conga, and afterhours folks were dropping into Burp Hollow, presumably to do more than the club's name implied. Over the hill on Ventura Boulevard, ex-vaudevillian Grace Hayes converted a barn into a nightclub with other vaudeville players as entertainers, to match the mood of comfortable spots like Ted Snyder's and Chasen's. She had an overnight sensation on her hands. Being the wife of Charlie Foy helped, of course, and friends such as Jimmy Cag-

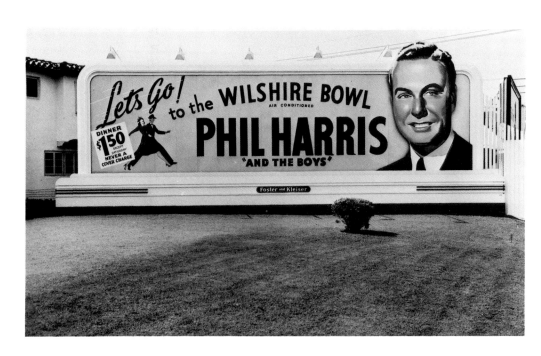

Above. The success of the Wilshire Bowl was due in large part to the presence of Phil Harris and ''The Boys,'' advertised here on a billboard along a Hollywood street.

Opposite above. The Beverly Hills branch of the Derby at Rodeo Drive and Wilshire Boulevard was a favorite hangout in the heart of the film colony.

Opposite below. Clark Gable and Carole Lombard happily pose at the ever-popular Brown Derby.

ney, Jane Wyman, and Jack LaRue relaxed under the protective eye of Grace, who banned photographers and autograph hounds from disturbing her gathering place. Impromptu performances by ''names'' assured Grace a full house night after night, and the interior, though simple, was said to be decorated solely by gifts from Grace's famous friends.

Across town in the suburb of South Gate, Ted Lewis opened at another new dance emporium called Topsy's, and Eddie Cantor, who guest emceed, made the drive out into the country with Jack Benny and Burns and Allen to greet the singer.

Smaller clubs seemed to saturate all of Hollywood, and nobody counted the endless list of locales that 1938 had available. When not occupied with a big evening at one of the larger spots around town, the stars scurried from one end of the city to the other, dancing, dining, and sipping alcoholic concoctions as nutty as a mixture of Pisco Brandy, passion fruit, and ice called the ''Surrealist's Surprise.'' The entertainment section of the local Beverly Hills newspaper gives an indication of the almost unbelievable selection of clubs in the area. A typical sampling might include the 41 Club on the site of the old Century Club on Beverly Boulevard, Billy Berg's Capri on Pico at La Cienega, Club Cercle down the street on Pico, Harry O'Day's, Two Harry's, the Hi Hat, where customers were treated to rides around the block in the Hi Hat taxi, Frank Sebastian's new enterprise, the

170

The opening of Earl Carroll's Theater-Restaurant on Sunset capped a decade of frantic nightlife in the cinema capital.

Cubanola, on LaBrea near Beverly, the Hollywood Rollerbowl, the Swanee Inn on LaBrea, Brittingham's Radio City Restaurant, Marcel Lamaze Restaurant on the site of the old Club Seville, Westwood Tropical Ice Gardens, and ad infinitum. As Hollywood was winding up another year, two clubs had plans to open simultaneously at the lucrative end-of-the-year session. Florentine Gardens and Earl Carroll's capped another banner year for cinema nightlife.

The superlatives that gushed over the opening of Broadway producer Earl Carroll's theater-restaurant on Sunset near Vine on December 26 were no idle chatter. The showman in the Ziegfeld tradition had conceived and built a nightclub of which even Hollywood had not conceived. On a tract of land strategically placed in the most active part of town, Carroll engaged architect Gordon Kaufman to build an auditorium capable of seating one thousand people in luxurious comfort. The result was a spectacular showplace that rivaled every nightclub in the world.

The decorative medium Carroll chose was an expansive system of lighting. The centerpiece of the system was a gilded, streamlined statue in the foyer, from which a fifty-foot neon tube wound its way to the black patent leather ceiling. From there, 6,200 feet of blue and gold neon tubes formed a luminous fringe undulating in graceful curves across the main floor, and ending in thirty-foot columns of light flanking the stage. The

171

172

stage itself was an eighty-foot double-revolving affair with an elevator. The east wall of the auditorium was covered in mock Australian oriental wood wallpaper shipped from England on the *Normandie*. The west wall was draped in green satin. Deep rose carpets covering the foyer and the six terraces in the main room were complemented by chairs and table settings of a lighter shade of pink. The bar in the foyer was hemmed by columns of glass tubes, backlit in soft hues. The grand staircase, the top of which was surmounted by the world's largest etched glass panel entitled *Young Ladies Aspiring for Stardom*, led to smoking rooms above. Flanking the glass mural were two female statues designed by Willy Pogany. The ladies' room was lined in soft peach lamb's wool, the dressing tables and chairs were upholstered in handwoven fabric in pastels, light green and cafe au lait, and the carpet, also handwoven, was colored dubonnet. The men's smoking room was finished in brown cork. The exterior of the building, edged in neon, supported a twenty-four-foot "painting in neon" of a woman's profile; a halo inscribed with "Through these portals pass the most beautiful girls in the world" skirted the portrait. On the adjoining outside wall, Carroll initiated the tradition of hanging concrete blocks inscribed with celebrities' autographs.

For the investors and members of the inner circle, a $1,000 membership fee guaranteed a lifetime cover charge and a reserved seat. The opening night celebra-

Opposite. Earl Carroll's interior reached a plateau of extravagance with patent leather ceilings, satin walls, and 6,200 feet of neon.

Above. Robert Taylor surveying Earl Carroll's opening-night pageant of beauties.

tion drew the cream of the Los Angeles and Hollywood social sets. First-nighters included Clark Gable and Carole Lombard, Marlene Dietrich, Tyrone Power, Sonja Henie, Bob Hope, Betty Grable, Jack Benny, Claudette Colbert, Robert Taylor, Constance Bennett, Daryl Zanuck, Jackie Coogan, Franchot Tone, Errol Flynn, David Selznick, Louis B. Mayer, Dolores Del Rio, Edgar Bergen, Jack Warner, W. C. Fields, Don Ameche, Walter Pidgeon, and dozens more. Klieg lights lit up the skies, and traffic along Sunset was jammed for more than two blocks. Fans thronged the entrance as limousine after limousine deposited Hollywood's finest. Inside, dinner was courtesy of Felix Ganio, late of the Trocadero, Vendome, and Waldorf-Astoria.

173

Ray Noble's orchestra provided the music for the stage revue, which opened with a skit entitled "Talent is What the Public Wants." Master of ceremonies Paul Gerrits introduced tableau after spectacular tableau. "The Blue Danube," "Candlelight," and "Tyrolean" numbers heaped a lavish helping of Carroll flair to a delighted audience. The sixty gorgeous showgirls in the cast flirted and bantered with the crowd in their nearly nude costumes, and managed to get Bob Hope, Jack Benny, Jimmy Durante, Errol Flynn, Milton Berle, Joe E. Brown, Walter Pidgeon, Don Ameche, Robert Taylor, and W. C. Fields on stage for a lively game of patty-cake. The finale, a sexy and saucy "Can-Can" ensemble, closed the evening to deafening applause. Carroll's

Earl Carroll's success inspired a movie version of his famed club as well as countless items promoting his landmark nightspot.

176

FRANK R. BRUNI'S

FLORENTINE Gardens   HOLLYWOOD

Above. A provocative damsel graces a Florentine Gardens program.

Opposite. The opening-night ad for Florentine Gardens heralded the club's amazing array of features.

unequivocal success insured him a permanent place in the Hollywood spectrum, and his showplace became the crowning jewel of nighttime diversion.

Florentine Gardens, a few short blocks away, bowed to a similar audience of well-wishers on December 28. Another massive structure holding 1,000 people, Guido Braccini's enterprise was geared to catch the business that Earl Carroll's turned away, and a six-course dinner priced at one dollar filled the place for dining and dancing. For the celebs who attended opening night, it was a brilliant affair featuring the Fanchon and Marco floor show and Emil Baffa's orchestra. The powder blue and gold furnishings were set against an interior suggesting an open-air garden, and the exterior, though described at the time as modern, was somewhat classical in its lines, with a bit of Hollywood Regency panache thrown in. Though its advertisements lauded it as an exotic setting of ancient Florence, the Gardens were hard-pressed to come up to the standards of Earl Carroll's intense display of luxury.

In time, Braccini's name was replaced by the initials N. T. G., which stood for Nils Thor Granlund, who took over the reins of the place after successfully running several big-time nightspots in New York. The sedate program was enhanced with glamour gals in the chorus line who revealed a bit more flesh than Braccini was used to, and customers lined up seven days a week to ogle and participate in the sophisticated stage show Granlund

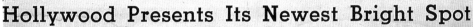

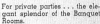

dreamed up. The garden concept was scrapped, and in its place producer Frank Bruni created a cosmopolitan ambiance akin to Carroll's on Sunset. The Venetian Room lounge disappeared, and in its place the Zanzibar Room opened. In later years, Florentine Gardens could claim on its roster of entertainers Sophie Tucker, Paul Whiteman, Dave Marshall, Harry Richman, and chorine Yvonne DeCarlo, who was plucked from the chorus for a career in movies.

The wrap-up of 1938 was a fast-paced hodgepodge of movie star comings and goings. A bowling and rollerskating craze erupted, filling alleys and rinks with the well-heeled sportsters. And for those seeking the ultimate in Southern California experiences, the al fresco Tropical Ice Gardens in Westwood opened right after Christmas for sun-worshipping ice-skaters. The New Year's crowd once again jammed the nighteries to capacity, the slickly renovated Troc breaking in its reopened dining room to the strains of Ted Fio Rito. Cotton snowballs were distributed at midnight, and promptly a battle broke out, with some stars soaking these favors in water or dipping them in butter before heaving them about the room. Another New Year's Eve under a heyday-Hollywood's belt.

The last year of the decade never looked better to the land of celluloid make-believe. Studio production was at its zenith. Nineteen thirty-nine was the year of *Gone with the Wind*, *My Little Chickadee*, *Mr. Smith Goes to Washington*, *The*

178

Above. Florentine Gardens at 5955
Hollywood Boulevard opened two days after
Earl Carroll's club several blocks away.

Opposite above. Bandleader Dave Marshall
proudly poses in his new Ford loaded with
Florentine Gardens chorus girls and, below,
on stage with his band.

Wizard of Oz, *Ninotchka*, *Stagecoach*, *Goodbye Mr. Chips*, and *Young Mr. Lincoln*. The town was loaded with tourists taking a peek at the myth they'd heard so much about, while newcomers flooded in at a steady rate, hoping to somehow repeat the Cinderella fable that had endured the passing decades.

The trades and gossip columns for the first of the year reported: the best-dressed gal at Earl Carroll's was Judith Garrett in a gown of white marquisette, décolleté bodice pleated and outlined in a shallow ruffle of net with sequins and silver sandals . . . *The 400 Peanut Vendors*, an organization of celebs who pined for a private night without the gaze of fans, were meeting at La Conga every Sunday night for a complimentary buffet and a night of rhumba-ing sponsored by twelve film personalities (opening night featured a real-life goober vendor roasting nuts at the door) . . . Marcel Lamaze opened his own place on the Strip and The Vendome closed its doors, reopening as Ruby Foo's, where dishes previewed for big name guests became the menu . . . Olivia DeHaviland hosted a dinner for the commanding officers of the San Pedro and San Diego naval bases at Victor Hugo's, and Harry Sugarman of Beverly Hills Tropics conquered new territory by opening a branch on Vine Street and turning over half the opening night's proceeds to the L.A. Coordinating Committee for German Refugees. And so it went for much of the year.

The one melancholy event in an other-

179

180

*Tropical Ice Gardens in Westwood was a
novel diversion for picture folk bent on relaxed
exercise warmed by the California sun.*

The burning of the Palomar Ballroom signaled the decade's end, while the Cocoanut Grove's annual New Year's bash ushered in a fresh decade of Hollywood nightlife.

wise prosperous year happened on October 2, when the Palomar Ballroom burned to the ground during an engagement by Charlie Barnet. The fire started during intermission, when a cloth lying on the equipment of a radio engineer burst into flames and sent 1,500 dancers scrambling for the exits. Although the band's instruments were destroyed along with the structure, no one was hurt except dance fans, who suffered the loss of their premier stomping grounds. The arrival of the New Year and a new decade seemed promising, though the war in Europe was taking an ominous turn. It had been a tremendous decade, full of losses and gratification. In Hollywood, movies had matured into an industry of almost inconceivable power and wealth, and the nightclub scene that had flourished in its wake reflected the city at its prime. It was a madcap society, bent on having the most of everything, and though it was far from over, it would never be quite the same as it was in the '30s.

181

THE FORTIES

The year 1940 brought forth one powerful burst of nightclub activity that would sustain the motion picture colony through its gradual demise in the period following the war. Hollywood, the sleepy suburb of a mere twenty-five years before, was now a town of mythic proportions. The hamlet of silent picture stars had spread out all over the Los Angeles area by the 1940s, and what was referred to as "Hollywood" was really meant to encompass anything having to do with the motion picture industry. Stars had settled down in Bel Air, Brentwood, and the Valley. Studios were established in all directions, from Culver City to Burbank. Spending millions was commonplace.

Two entertainment ventures debuted in January. The first was Casa Mañana, which revamped Frank Sebastian's Cotton Club into a moderne dance ballroom. With the demise of the Palomar, Casa Mañana took up the lead, and top bands added it to their agenda as one of the West Coast "musts." Skinnay Ennis opened the place to a hall full of big band devotees, who were still plentiful in the movie colony.

On the Strip, entrepreneur Billy Wilkerson was at it again—this time, planning another legendary showplace of magnificent proportions on the site of the old Club Seville. Ciro's opened at the end of January, 1940, and, as was the case with his other enterprise, it was an instant hit. The stars, abandoning the recent trend of staying home, flocked to Hollywood's newest in-spot. What greeted them was a sophisticated exterior facade by George Vernon Russell and inside a Baroque confection by interior designer Tom Douglas. Under the supervision of Wilkerson, Mr. Douglas created the latest in Hollywood glamour, with walls draped in heavy, ribbed silk, dyed pale reseda green, and a ceiling painted American Beauty red. The stars sank themselves into wall sofas also of silk, dyed to match the ceiling. Bronze columns and urns served as lighting fixtures that flanked the bandstand. Everywhere, the endless attention of a Wilkerson business was evident. Ads preceding the opening were a daily occurrence in the *Hollywood Reporter*, wherein readers were reminded that: "Everybody that's anybody will be at Ciro's." And pretty much everybody in Hollywood turned up for the two openings on subsequent nights. Emil Coleman's orchestra initiated the bandstand, and it was reported that as a tip a bartender received five shares of Grand National stock. For weeks after the opening, the only place to be was Ciro's. Post-premiere parties, benefits, and birthdays were all celebrated there. Certainly one of the oddest occasions in its early days was a fashion show by a local furrier who paraded models in his expensive pelts accompanied by a live animal with the same fur she wore. Beavers, leopards, and minks got a firsthand view of Hollywood nightlife in the hallowed halls of Ciro's.

The latest hotspot naturally was under surveillance by the leading columnists,

Lucille Ball and Desi Arnaz

and Hedda and Louella camped out many an evening to inform the public of Veronica Lake's alcoholic bouts, who Judy Garland was palling around with, and the clothes worn by Hollywood's finest. The fights matched the fame of the club, and barely a week went by that some leading man was not banned for causing a ruckus. Lana Turner named it her favorite haunt, and with high-powered endorsements such as hers, Ciro's entered the realm of legend, which it held for almost two decades. After several years, as was Wilkerson's habit, he abandoned Ciro's and went on to establish La Rue down the street. In his place, Herman Hover took over the reins, and once again the club made a hit with the film colony, sustaining its reputation through the McCarthy era.

The practice many movie stars made of investing or lending their names to various clubs, restaurants, and dance halls was not new to the '40s. Fatty Arbuckle's, Ted Snyder's Hawaiian Paradise, the Embassy Club, and others all had backing from the motion picture community. Now, it seemed, everyone wanted in.

On May 3, Bing Crosby, Bob Hope, Fred MacMurray, Jimmy Fiddler, Johnny Weismuller, Ken Murray, Rudy Vallee, Tony Martin, Errol Flynn, and Vic Erwin banded together to produce the Pirate's Den on LaBrea near Beverly, the site on which the Three Little Pigs and Sebastian's Cubanola had been. As its name implied, the atmosphere was Jolly Roger, Hollywood-style. From the moment you

185

Opposite. At 8433 Sunset, Ciro's facade, designed by architect George Vernon Russell, reflected Hollywood's sophisticated tastes of 1940.

Above and right. The interior of Ciro's was a baroque confection of silk sofas and walls painted reseda green and American beauty red.

186

*Left. Olivia DeHavilland and Robert Payne
scurry through Ciro's doors.*

*Above. Ciro's opening-night ad emphasized
the formality of the new nightspot.*

Above. Ciro's interior changed as frequently as its owners. Shown is the mid-'40s dance floor.

Ciro's bar circa 1941.

Above. Entrance to the Pirate's Den at 335 N. LaBrea and the scream diploma that freed female customers from the brig.

Opposite left. Paulette Goddard and Charlie Chaplin at Ciro's.

entered to the clanging of ship's bells, the Pirate's Den guaranteed a mad and merry time. Female patrons were ''abducted'' by bands of roving swashbucklers (who doubled as waiters) and thrown into the brig on some phony charge. Then the only way of escape was by screaming until one of the brigands yelled: ''Turn her loose, she's having more fun than we are!,'' at which point she was awarded a scream diploma. Imbibing at the Skull and Bones bar on one of ''six mystifying drinks,'' customers were treated to nonstop antics by the swarm of pirates who staged mock battles at any convenient moment. A pirate crossing the floor with a tray of eating utensils might find himself sprawled on the floor, tripped by another corsair, and a ''hanging'' would ensue. Another offender had the whip administered by ''Bullwhip Garur,'' who realistically lashed a waiter with his fifteen-foot bullwhip. After the punishments, the bodies were disposed of in a wheelbarrow, and the deck was cleared for another confrontation. During the war years, a bottle gallery was provided for the hurling of empty flagons at mockups of Tojo, Hitler, and Il Duce.

Another Hollywood big name renovated a house near the Garden of Allah and admitted guests only through an odd policy. Preston Sturges, producer and playwright, got a place of his own after his involvement with Ted Snyder's. So Players', named after the actors' club in New York's Gramercy Park, opened quietly in the summer of 1940. In keep-

189

Above. Preston Sturges's Players' rested
against the hills at 8225 Sunset Boulevard.

The intimacy of the Bar of Music at 7351 Beverly Boulevard reflected the small-club atmosphere in vogue in 1940s Hollywood.

ing with its somewhat eccentric owner, Players' would close its doors when Sturges wanted to entertain his own pals, and, when the public was admitted, if someone looked out of line he was bounced out. The restaurant was on two levels, and when, after the first season, it showed a loss, Sturges closed it and substituted a music and dance area called the Playroom, which had a gala opening the first part of 1942. Writers and stars made it a home base, and it flourished with regulars Howard Hughes, Barbara Stanwyck, Orson Welles, and Humphrey Bogart. Superb food was its trademark and the Blue Room its formal dining area. Sturges even installed a barber shop on the mezzanine level. In time, his private rendezvous—which never seemed to break even—fell from favor; and, despite remodelings and renovations, by the end of the war more tourists were likely to be found in Players' than anyone recognizable as a star.

Several similar clubs of importance, like the Bar of Music on Beverly Boulevard, opened in the time between summer and the arrival in the fall of the town's replacement for the Palomar: the Palladium. Halloween night saw the Palladium fling open its doors to the crowds who had gathered on Sunset for the grand opening. The million-dollar ballroom had everyone gaping, and the press outdid itself in coining superlatives for it. Names such as the Temple of Terpsichore, Super Ballroom, and Everybody's Night Club fittingly described the Palladium, and,

191

192

Above. The Palladium across the street from Earl Carroll's on Sunset was the favored dance spot of movie stars and Big Bands alike.

Opposite. The massive Palladium dance floor accommodated 7,500 dancers and was presided over by Tommy Dorsey on opening night.

once inside, no one was disappointed by the promise of the descriptions. The creation of Frank Don Riha, who was also the decorator of Earl Carroll's across the street, the ballroom was the ultimate in sophistication, with a kidney-shaped dance floor designed to conform with the dancers' circular rotation and cushioned with cork to alleviate fatigue. The balcony overlooking the entire ballroom was reached by wide, sweeping staircases flanked by stylized dancing fems symbolizing the spirit of dance and gaiety. Those entering from the porte cochere wound their way through halls faced with redwood boards in a perforated grille pattern lit from behind. Next came a bar and circular cocktail room with a redwood dome of fifty feet in diameter. The cavernous ballroom proper had 12,000 square feet of dancing area to accommodate 7,500 dancers and 1,000 diners. The color scheme was silver and pearly gray, accented by coral; and on either side of the stage two immense lucite panels etched with feminine beauties stood at attention. The college under-age crowd could belly-up to a 200-foot-long milk bar finished in emerald. Riha's specially created "Color Symphonies" lighting syncopated in harmony with the dance music, drifting from shadows of blue and orchid for waltzes to *Sangre de boeuf* for sensuous rhumbas.

Tommy Dorsey, on his trombone, blew the first blast to be heard in the Palladium at 8:30 P.M., and at 9:45 Dorothy Lamour, alongside Dorsey, cut a ribbon

194

Barbara Stanwyck and Gary Cooper share dinner chatter at the Palladium.

draped with orchids, signaling the formal dedication. An estimated 10,000 jammed the place to the rafters, while, outside, searchlights combed the skies as hundreds more surged to get a glimpse of the parade of stars that arrived. Following Dorsey were Kay Kyser, Artie Shaw, Glen Miller, Larry Clinton, and Glen Gray—whose engagements confirmed the dance hall as the nation's premier showplace.

Glen Miller's appearance seven months after the opening was indicative of the Palladium's drawing power. Miller, who was in town to film Fox's *Sun Valley Serenade*, invited the entire cast as his guests, and, not wanting to be left out, Hollywood phoned in reservations for Bing Crosby, Bob Hope, Alice Faye, Phil Harris, Betty Grable, George Raft, Lana Turner, Tony Martin, Judy Garland, Dave Rose, Connie Boswell, Rudy Vallee, the Andrews Sisters, and Abbott and Costello.

The Palladium, Ciro's, and the other draws of 1940 collectively closed the door on what seemed to be an outmoded style of club, represented by the Troc and the Clover Club. A series of raids in January and November put a damper on their operations, and in the case of the Clover Club it was a terminal notice. No longer would the cream and gold walls reverberate to the sound of slots and roulette wheels, while band members and employees shuffled past gun-toting guards on their way to work. The underworld figures Willie Bioff, Bugsy Siegel, Mic-

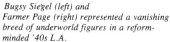
Bugsy Siegel (left) and
Farmer Page (right) represented a vanishing
breed of underworld figures in a reform-
minded '40s L.A.

key Cohen, and Farmer Page were being transferred to Nevada, and the gambling that replaced the backroom variety was more often out-in-the-open horseracing.

The clubs of the 1940s tended toward the intimate and refined, more like an evening at home, which was what many of the stars opted for rather than all-night assaults and blasting bands.

The town's premier imposter, Mike Romanoff, epitomized this trend in his celebrity-backed restaurant on fashionable Rodeo Drive in Beverly Hills. Romanoff's opened at 325 North Rodeo on December 19, 1940, and the "Emperor," as he was known to his long list of friends, had finagled through pal Harry Crocker $7,500 each from a host of movie folk that included Robert Benchley, Cary Grant, Daryl Zanuck, and John Hay Whitney. The supposed "cousin of the late czar" offered choice food and shooed away tourists and autograph hounds who might disturb his imperial "guests." The orange, green, and yellow wallpaper was his personal choice, as was the general layout. For select regulars and stockholders, the first seven banquettes on the left, opposite the bar, were reserved, and anyone entering the restaurant had to pass right by them. Bogart ate there almost daily, but Romanoff preferred to dine alone, often attended only by his two bulldogs, Socrates and Confucius. Regulars could stay at a table as long as they wished, often playing backgammon, gin rummy, or just chatting. Unknowns and offenders of the proprietor's code were

195

196

ROMANOFFS

banned or told to leave. Decorations were on loan from various contributors, and Romanoff's settled comfortably into Prince Mike's first restaurant venture, with a tidy profit reaped on top of it all.

At the end of 1940, another much-anticipated club was in preparation for a New Year's opening, but it missed the gala holiday by just three days. Mocambo bowed to the public on Friday, January 3, 1941, at the site of the old Club Versailles on the Strip. The ten-dollar opening night tariff hardly slowed the steady procession of stars parading under the canopy into a room that was to be the setting for a decade's worth of extraordinary glamour. Owners Felix Young and ex-agent Charlie Morrisson, who had never run a nightclub before, created an extraordinary background for their restaurant, which was described as ''a cross between a somewhat decadent Imperial Rome, Salvador Dali, and a birdcage.'' Allusions to a Mexican motif, as suggested by the name, were carried out in a ''medley of soft blue, flamboyant terra cotta, and scintillating silver.'' Splashed on the walls were paintings by Jane Berlandina, and scattered discreetly along the walls were huge baroque tin flowers. Columns were painted a flaming red, and harlequins scampered on them. Rows of oversized ball fringe decorated lacquered trees, and striped patterns were everywhere. The crowning point of the club, however, was a dazzling aviary of live birds that everyone was talking about. The birds, in fact, almost caused Mo-

Above. Romanoff's interior was the inner sanctum of Prince Mike (foreground) who also chose the orange, green, and yellow wallpaper.

Opposite. Prince Romanoff regally adorned his menu.

Above. Anita Colby and Humphrey Bogart at Mocambo.

Opposite. Prince Mike Romanoff observing his ritual lunch with pet pooches Socrates and Confucius.

cambo not to open. The twenty-one parakeets, four love birds, four macaws, and a cockatoo were thought to be damaged by exposure to nighttime noise, and local animal lovers wanted them protected. However, owner Morrisson assured everyone that the birds were enjoying themselves, and he even kept the drapes pulled during the day, to allow the birds extra rest.

The $100,000 establishment was a nightclub's nightclub. Every evening was star night, including the presence of many of Hollywood's homebodies, who made it their occasional haunt. Even competitors dropped in for fun and food. Prince Mike Romanoff slipped in from time to time, on one occasion taking a punch from agent William Burnside and declaring afterward: ''I wish they had let me go for just a minute, and I would have annihilated him.'' Even a partial list of those who turned up at Mocambo was amazing for its time: Marlene Dietrich with Jean Gabin; Judy Garland with husband David Rose; Lana Turner and Tony Martin; Myrna Loy and Arthur Hornblow celebrating their divorce together; Carole and Clark Gable; Lucille Ball and Desi Arnaz out rhumba'ing; Louis Mayer; Reggie Gardiner; Hedy LaMarr; Barbara Hutton; Cary Grant; Cole Porter; Irving Berlin and Rosalind Russell. At one table might be Franchot Tone, Henry Fonda, Jimmy Stewart, and Burgess Meredith; while, at another, Douglas Fairbanks, Jr., could be found deep in conversation with Norma Shearer. With such a highly

199

Mocambo, described as a nightclub's nightclub, opened at 8588 Sunset on January 3, 1941.

The extravagant Mocambo interior in full swing.

202

Maria Montez makes a dramatic Mocambo entrance.

charged room of celebrities, the fights were inevitable. Errol Flynn, in one famous altercation, slugged Jimmy Fiddler, who had slurred him, and promptly got a fork in the ear from the columnist's wife.

Parties were another extravagance that Mocambo easily accommodated. Oil heiress Elinore Machris gave a $30,000 party to announce her remarriage, only to be topped by Lana Turner, who gave a $40,000 birthday party for her husband.

Andre was lured away from "21" in New York as maitre 'd. Phil Ohman, long a fixture at the Trocadero, was the house bandleader, and August Roche, a twenty-year veteran of continental cooking, presented the pampered stars with culinary treats. Mocambo, as fan-magazine reporter Lloyd Pantages observed, ". . . is a place in Hollywood which looks like Hollywood—magnificent, luxurious, exotic and unique." With the opening of Mocambo, the last great heyday of Hollywood nightclubbing was in full swing. Together with Romanoff's, Ciro's, the Cocoanut Grove, the Palladium, and Earl Carroll's, the pace for the rest of the '40s was set. With the exception of the bigger draws like the Palladium and Earl Carroll's, most clubs of the decade tended toward the intimate and refined, dismissing the loud bands and the novelties of the 1930s. Subdued and sophisticated were the call words.

There was a surplus of lesser draws amidst the stellar accomplishments along the strip and in the exclusive Beverly

Bathed in glorious Mocambo light are George Jessel and Lois Andrews.

Hills colony. Rhum Boogie on Highland near Melrose latched onto the rhumba craze with Ceepee Johnson and his tom-toms delighting dancers at his holiday opening. Alice Faye joined the band-wagon of celebrity owners when she lent her name and cash to a former diner on Wilshire and San Vicente shaped like a streamlined train. Together with partners Harry Sugarman (of Tropic's fame) and brother Bill Faye, she made the Club Car a rousing success for a few seasons. Its January 23 opening announced a 24-hour policy, and the eye-catcher here was M.G.M. set designer Merrill Pye's incorporation of Hollywood star autographs into wallpaper, draperies, and aprons of the servers.

Down the street on the Miracle Mile portion of Wilshire, the Wilshire Bowl consistently packed 'em onto the medium-sized dance floor, presided over by Maestro Phil Harris. The Wilshire Bowl, which had been around since the mid-'30s, was as popular as ever in the early '40s, especially for comedians, who made it a popular hangout.

Among the other contenders opening in the spring of 1941 were Charlie Foy's on Ventura Boulevard, out in the Valley; and, farther down the road, Harry Carroll, songwriter of hits like ''Trail of the Lonesome Pine'' and ''I'm Always Chasing Rainbows,'' opened Tin Pan Alley for refugees of the ''Big Apple'' songster crowd. Closer to Hollywood, Slim and Slam, the original Flat Foot Floogie Boys, played the Swanee Inn on LaBrea, a

203

Above. Errol Flynn, Nora Eddington, and John Dekker share a laugh at Mocambo.

Opposite. Vera Hruba Ralston and John Wayne take a spin on the Mocambo's dance floor.

showcase for "Sepia" entertainment. Dubbed "Harlem in Hollywood," the King Cole Swingsters were also a featured act. Along the same lines, Little Eva on Sunset revamped the former Bagdad niterie into a slick, domed dining room and dance floor, offering Southern-style dinners, entertainment, and decor of scenes illustrating *Uncle Tom's Cabin* and steamboats on the Mississippi. Billie Holiday headlined in the fall of 1941 at Cafe Society, in the unlikely locale of the San Fernando Valley. Another renovated club, Cafe Society was short-lived, though the fact that it even survived showed interest in sophisticated black entertainment. The Bal Tabarin in Gardena and the Stork Club on Western also served as sources of "Colored Revues," and presumably they were safe enough for white audiences to show up. Oddly enough, within easy reach of just about any Hollywood resident was the real thing on Central Avenue. A hotbed of talent and entertainment, Central Avenue—just south of downtown—had for almost twenty years served as an entertainment focus for the black community. Relegated to primarily black neighborhoods, visiting "Sepia" bands and entertainers were forced to find hotel accommodations "among their own," and the Dunbar Hotel at 43rd and Central served as the meeting place for the greatest group of black talent in America. The street had established itself in the 1920s, and by the early '40s it hopped with activity. The Last Word and the Club Alabam sat next

205

206

Above. Club Zombie and other clubs throughout filmland were kept under the watchful eye of police during the '40s, halting illegal activity rampant in the '30s.

Opposite. Like Harlem in New York, Central Avenue and its environs were fertile ground for some of the best entertainment viewable by celebs making the trek south of downtown Los Angeles.

to the Dunbar in the center of the action. Here, the street reverberated with music. For those venturing to this side of town, a visit to the clubs could net Duke Ellington or Cab Calloway at ringside, enjoying a chorus line, orchestra, and floor show.

Further down the road in Compton, the Plantation at 108th Street billed itself as ''California's largest Harlem nightclub.'' It attracted the top black talent visiting town. In many ways, the performers that showcased on Central Avenue, far from Hollywood's glitter, outshined the prefabricated shows white audiences were fed. Central Avenue nurtured jam sessions and dance routines the hoi polloi of cinemaland never got to see. But for those who made the trip, the reward was talent at its uninhibited best.

On December 7, 1941, Hollywood and the rest of the world felt the shockwaves of war, and the entertainment capital of the world entered its final round of brilliant nightlife. The movie community, responding to the national crisis, had mobilized immediately. Studios trumped up security, leading stars took off for bond drives, and, for a while, nightclub activity almost ceased. But as the realization of the needs of the war effort impinged on a certain amount of entertainment activity, the clubs and restaurants in and around Hollywood began to fill again for fund-raising efforts. The sight of stars on their nightly rounds was a great morale booster for servicemen craving the normalcy of life back home, and so the momentary lapse in business was

207

...Farewell To 1940!
And A Toast To 1941!
WITH

FREDDY MARTIN

HIS OWN ENTERTAINERS
AND A GREAT GALAXY OF STARS AND REVELERS
AT THE

Gala New Year's Eve Party

Tuesday Evening, December 31st

IN THE

Ambassador "Cocoanut Grove"

A magnificent souvenir for every lady—a baby Panda
(note picture below), but bigger than a healthy baby.
Dinner or supper de luxe will be served throughout the evening.
Novelties and noise makers for everyone.
$15.00 per person plus State and Federal Tax $1.11—Total $16.11.
Please make reservations on card enclosed.
All reservations will receive from the Maître d'Hotel
a table number definitely establishing location in the Grove.

Mine!
What a wonderful
Souvenir!

1941

replenished by the time New Year's rolled around.

The huge influx of servicemen and war workers to California's Southland provided Hollywood with a massive patronage never seen before. Barring blackouts and gas rationing, swingshifters flocked to Earl Carroll's, where specially priced shows catered to the late-night workers. The newcomers jammed the dance spots from the Zenda Ballroom downtown to Casino Gardens in Ocean Park. In most places, servicemen were admitted at a discount; and some establishments even eliminated the tariff for men in uniform. By October of 1942, the Hollywood community, headed by Bette Davis and John Garfield, had organized studio heads, unions, and guilds into creating an enlisted serviceman's center staffed by Hollywood's finest. Bolstered with funds donated by Ciro's and Columbia Studios after the premiere of *Talk of the Town*, the committee leased the property of a former night-joint known as The Barn, at 1451 Cahuenga near Sunset. The various guilds donated their talent and materials to renovate the structure into the Hollywood Canteen. Studio artists and cartoonists decorated the walls, Cary Grant donated a piano, Jack Warner provided linoleum, and countless hours of work by studio plumbers, electricians, and carpenters transformed the dusty structure into a cozy, Western-themed nightclub. On opening night, October 3, stars paid $100 a seat to watch the festivities and the parade of servicemen who

Opposite. Freddy Martin at the Cocoanut Grove insured a star-packed New Year's in 1941.

Top. George Raft and friend at Crillon.

Bottom. Louis Hayward and Ida Lupino chat at Mocambo.

Tom Breneman initiated his "Breakfast in Hollywood" program at Sardi's, later moving it to Vine Street where evening entertainment was featured as well.

Opposite. Bogie and Bacall dine at Mocambo.

Above. The Hollywood Canteen on Cahuenga near Sunset.

Left. Fans gather to watch the stars arrive for duty at the Canteen.

Opposite. Ginger Rogers and Fred MacMurray cheerily sign autographs for Canteen servicemen.

crammed the hall. After opening speeches by Bette and John, and the banter of Abbott and Costello, sailors, soldiers, and marines jostled through the entrance, above which was inscribed "Through these portals pass the most beautiful uniforms in the world"—an obvious borrowing from Earl Carroll's famed motto. Inside, the talk of war was discouraged. Kay Kyser, Rudy Vallee, and Duke Ellington played for dancers, and everything was on the house. Carole Landis, Loretta Young, Irene Dunne, Marlene Dietrich, Joan Crawford, and Rita Hayworth were but a few of the hostesses who danced with the boys in uniform. Male stars bussed dishes, and even mothers of the stars took turns serving coffee and sandwiches and washing dishes. The dance floor, however, was where the action was. Betty Grable was clocked dancing with 42 men in eight minutes. Autographs were liberally handed out, and, for the duration, the Hollywood Canteen was the hottest spot in town for anybody involved in the military service.

The obvious advantages of the Canteen guaranteed it a full house every night, from its 6 P.M. opening to its midnight closing. The weekly food bill averaged $3,000, and nightly attendance reached 1,200 men per shift. Within six months, 125 name bands had played over five hundred hours of dance music. Over six hundred top stars had entertained on stage, and the seemingly endless appetites of the guests consumed fifty thousand pieces of cake, six thousand gallons

214

Left. The Andrew Sisters give it their all at the Canteen.

Above. Mickey Rooney lets loose on the drums in a Hollywood canteen appearance.

Opposite. Greer Garson poses with some Canteen friends.

216

of coffee, and seventy-two Thanksgiving turkeys. The myth of Hollywood became a reality for the endless streams of servicemen until the Canteen closed its doors for good at the end of the war.

For the stars on their nocturnal rounds, the nightlife continued at a breathtaking pace. The shadow of war seemed only to accentuate their activity. The Strip still held forth as the premier spot to see and be seen, but the dance halls were equally popular in the star draw, from the Palladium in Hollywood to the Trianon in South Gate. Uniforms were everywhere. With production at an all-time peak, studios were equally anxious to have their stars in the limelight, and a well-documented soiree at the Cocoanut Grove or Ciro's kept profiles high. Meanwhile, in Beverly Hills, Billy Wilkerson was busy opening another investment: L'Aiglon, which turned out to be short-lived but well attended by the crowds that followed Wilkerson enterprises. On Vine, in the El Capitan Theater, Ken Murray presented the first of his ''Blackouts'' series, which combined the busty zaniness of Marie Wilson with a nonstop vaudeville show. Described as a rich dressing of girls, laughs, and thrills, the blending of animal acts, dance duos, and comedy skits gave the Hollywood colony an opportunity to laugh some of their wartime

Top. The Strip in the '40s included Mocambo, Crillon, Trocadero, and LaRue within walking distance of each other.

Bottom. Victor Mature and party at Ciro's.

thoughts away. Around the corner at Sardi's, another showman attracted large crowds in the morning hours. Tom Breneman broadcast his national radio program from the famed restaurant for several years until he moved to Vine, eventually settling in at the site of the Hollywood Tropics. Tom was a hit with the tourists, and celebrities dropped in from time to time for breakfast and to plug their latest movie.

As 1942 came to a close, Hollywood was still the magical place the world envisioned. Its image and the nightly meanderings of famous filmites boosted the morale of the entire nation, which equated its exquisite trappings and extravagant surroundings with a country that had the best to offer. From 1943 until the end of the war, the pace of new niteries opening stabilized with the establishments that had opened in the previous five years, gleaning most of the star trade. One exception was the ever-busy Billy Wilkerson, who opened yet another swank spot on the Strip—LaRue—in April of 1944. Not as extravagant as some of his former enterprises, it nonetheless became a trademark of discriminating taste and a hangout for the well-heeled Screenland celebrity. Because it was primarily a restaurant, LaRue was more of a gathering place than a niterie loaded with action, which

217

Above. Cary Grant and Ava Gardner lunch at the Brown Derby.

Below. The war years at the Derby brought out patriotic menus and a new Los Feliz branch.

218

Above. Casa Mañana, where Frank Sebastian's Cotton Club once held forth, hopped to name bands during Hollywood's war years.

Opposite above. A surprised Rita Hayworth dines with manager Bo Roos at LaRue.

Opposite below. Slapsy Maxie's capitalized on mayhem in its original location at 7165 Beverly Boulevard and its later locale at the old Wilshire Bowl.

perfectly suited a grown-up Hollywood.

By 1945, with the war's ending imminent, Hollywood and its social scene were on the verge of dramatic changes that would alter forever the business of motion pictures and the equally serious business of nightclub entertainment. True, Mocambo, Ciro's, Earl Carroll's, and the Cocoanut Grove were packed. A booth at the Brown Derby might take connections, but the changing structure of the studio system and the even more threatening specter of a new medium— television—were slowly entering a scene that had undergone a drastic upheaval. With a world war under its belt, and studio pressure absent from a star's personal life, sometimes it was easier to stay home and socialize with an intimate group of friends rather than make the rounds of nitespots. Another evident change was a shift in taste from the highly visible clubs loaded with photographers to smaller, more intimate quarters designed to insulate rather than exploit a star's presence. It was a trend that had been developing slowly over the previous decade.

Yet another factor in the decline of nightlife was the presence of a reform mayor in City Hall, who took a tough stance against crime syndicates in the city and flushed out most of the gambling activity, transferring it, and the money it procured, to the small Nevada desert town of Las Vegas. The big-name talent that had appeared in Hollywood for going rates was suddenly given the opportunity to perform in Vegas casinos at unheard-of

prices, which the gambling emporiums could easily afford to pay. Local clubs didn't stand a chance when faced with those odds. For the dance halls, the height of the Big Band era had reached its zenith in the mid-'40s, and by the end of the decade it, too, would be the victim of changing tastes, emptying the large ballrooms once filled with dancers.

The process of Hollywood's nightclub demise was a gradual one, but clearly VJ Day marked the beginning of the end. Just as the movies continued to make record-breaking attendance through 1946, Ciro's and Mocambo, the two most popular spots, also managed to pack in the crowds, something they would accomplish for several more years. When Earl Carroll died in a plane crash in 1948, his theater on Sunset closed, ending that type of big dinner show in Hollywood forever. Attendance at other nightclubs slowly dropped off, and in a short time it seemed that hardly anyone was doing the town. An occasional party might light the glow of former times, but the energy just didn't seem to be there.

Hollywood's golden era was laid to rest with the McCarthy era. But the years since its birth had been a roller-coaster ride of fantastic proportions. The nightclub era saw the greatest talent in the world on display nightly for more than thirty years. The magic sensation of stars on parade at night stirred the imaginations of millions of fans who never tired of seeing *their* favorite stars in glamorous trappings they themselves would

219

220

Above. The Derby, joined in 1941 by the Los Feliz branch, remained extremely popular with the stars. Posing at the Hollywood Derby are George Raft, Betty Grable, Virginia Gilmore, and Fritz Lang.

Left. The Aragon Ballroom dances in Ocean Park and the Blackouts at the El Capitan Theater were popular war-years entertainment.

never wear. The clubs were showcases, places to be seen and to rendezvous at with friends in the industry. They were places to show off unheard-of wealth, to settle arguments, or to indulge in exotic food. But most of all, they were Hollywood itself, that mythic kingdom to get lost in when the world became all too real.

221

Eddie Cantor and Marlene Dietrich pose for a Canteen Christmas portrait.

BOOKS

Anger, Kenneth. *Hollywood Babylon*. Sun Valley, Id.: Straight Arrow Books, 1975.

Basten, Fred. *Santa Monica Bay: The First Hundred Years*. Corona, Ca.: Douglas-West Publishers, 1974.

——. *Beverly Hills: Portrait of a Fabled City*. Corona, Ca.: Douglas-West Publishers, 1975.

Bradley, Bill. *Commercial Los Angeles*. Glendale, Ca.: Interurban Press, 1981.

Brownlow, Kevin. *The Parade's Gone By*. New York: Alfred A. Knopf, 1968.

——, and Kobal, John. *Hollywood—The Pioneers*. New York: Alfred A. Knopf, 1979.

Burk, Margaret T. *Are the Stars Out Tonight?* Wellesley, Mass.: Round Table West, 1980.

Burke, Tony. *Palm Springs—Why I Love You*. Palmesa, 1978.

Calloway, Cab, and Rollins, Bryant. *Of Minnie the Moocher and Me*. Thomas Y. Crowell Co., 1976.

Carr, Harry. *Los Angeles*. Pasadena, Ca.: D. Appleton-Century Co., 1935.

Clark, David I. *Los Angeles, A City Apart*. Woodland Hills, Ca.: Windsor Publications, 1981.

Cohen, Michael Mickey. *Mickey Cohen: In My Own Words*. Englewood Cliffs, N.J.: Prentice-Hall, 1975.

Curtis, James. *Between Flops*. New York: Harcourt Brace Jovanovich, 1982.

Davies, Marion. *The Times We Had*. New York: Bobbs-Merrill Co., 1975.

Driggs, Frank, and Lewine, Harris. *Black Beauty, White Heat*. New York: William Morrow & Co., 1982.

Finch, Christopher, and Rosenkrantz, Linda. *Gone Hollywood*. New York: Doubleday & Co., 1979.

Gebhard, David, and Von Breton, Harriet. *Los Angeles in the '30s*. Layton, Ut.: Peregrine Smith, 1975.

Graham, Sheila. *The Garden of Allah*. New York: Crown Publishers, 1970.

Hancock, Ralph. *Fabulous Boulevard*. New York: Funk & Wagnalls Co., 1949.

Haskins, Jim. *The Cotton Club*. New York: Random House, 1977.

Haver, Ronald. *David O. Selznick's Hollywood*. New York: Alfred A. Knopf, 1980.

Henstell, Bruce. *Los Angeles: An Illustrated History*. New York: Alfred A. Knopf, 1980.

——. *Sunshine and Wealth*. San Francisco: Chronicle Books, 1985.

Houston, Bob. *Sinning in Hollywood*. Marcell Rodd, 1943.

Kobal, John. *Rita Hayworth*. New York: W. W. Norton & Co., 1977.

Latham, Aaron. *Crazy Sundays: F. Scott Fitzgerald in Hollywood*. New York: Viking Press, 1971.

Lee, James. *Hollywood Agent*. Macaulay Co., 1937.

Loos, Anita. *Kiss Hollyood Good-By*. New York: Viking Press, 1974.

Lord, Jack, and Hoff, Lloyd. *How to Sin in Hollywood*. Richard F. Guggenheim, 1940.

Milland, Ray. *Wide-Eyed in Babylon*. Sun Valley, Id.: Straight Arrow Books, 1974.

Moran, Tom, and Sewell, Tom. *Fantasy by the Sea*. Venice, Ca.: Beyond Baroque Foundation, 1979.

Morella, Joe, and Epstein, Edward. *Lana*. Secaucus, N.J.: Citadel Press, 1971.

——. *The ''It'' Girl*. New York: Delacorte Press, 1976.

Murray, Ken. *The Body Merchant*. Ward Ritchie Press, 1976.

Niven, David. *Bring on the Empty Horses*. New York: G. P. Putnam's Sons, 1975.

Otis, Johnny. *Listen to the Lambs*. New York: W. W. Norton & Co., 1968.

Phillips, Cabell. *From the Crash to the Blitz, 1929–1939*. New York: Macmillan Co., 1969.

Rosten, Leo. *Hollywood: The Movie Colony*. New York: Harcourt, Brace & Co., 1941.

Shippey, Lee. *The Los Angeles Book*. New York: Houghton Mifflin Co., 1950.

Skolsky, Sidney. *Don't Get Me Wrong—I Love Hollywood*. New York: G. P. Putnam's Sons, 1975.

Stanton, Jeffrey, and Del Zoppo, Annette. *Venice, California, 1904–1930*. Stockton, Ca.: ARS Publications, 1973.

Swindell, Larry. *Screwball*. New York: William Morrow & Co., 1975.

Thomas, Bob. *Thalberg*. New York: Doubleday & Co., 1969.

Torrence, Bruce. *Hollywood: The First 100 Years*. Hollywood Chamber of Commerce and Pike Enterprises, 1979.

Walker, Alexander. *Rudolph Valentino*. Briarcliff Manor, N.Y.: Stein & Day, 1976.

Walker, Leo. *The Wonderful Era of the Great Dance Bands*. New York: Doubleday & Co., 1964.

Warren, Doug. *The Hollywood Reporter Movieland Guide*. Hollywood Reporter, 1979.

Webb-Herrick, Elisabeth. *Curious California Customs*. Pacific Carbon & Printing Co., 1935.

Westmore, Frank, and Davidson, Muriel. *The Westmores of Hollywood*. Philadelphia: J. B. Lippincott Co., 1976.

Wilkerson, Tichi, and Borie, Marcia. *The Hollywood Reporter: The Golden Years*. Putnam Publishing Group, 1984.

Wolsey, Serge. *Call House Madam*. Martin Tudordale Corp., 1942.

Woon, Basil. *Incredible Land*. New York: Liveright, 1933.

WPA Guide to Los Angeles. Work Projects Administration, 1941.

PERIODICALS

Architect and Engineer
Architects and Builders Magazine
Architectural Forum
Architectural Record
Beverly Hills Citizen
Business Week
California Arts and Architecture
Cinema Arts
Collier's
Daily Variety
Electrical West
Esquire
Holiday
Hollywood
Hollywood Citizen News, The

222

Hollywood Life
Hollywood Magazine
Hollywood Reporter, The
Hollywood Spectator
Hotel Management
Jone's Magazine
Life
Look
Los Angeles Daily Journal, The
Los Angeles Daily News
Los Angeles Examiner
Los Angeles Free Press
Los Angeles Magazine
Los Angeles Times
Motion Picture Classics
Motion Picture Magazine
Movie and Radio Guide
New York Times
Pacific Coast Record
Photoplay
Pic
Pictorial California
Restaurant Management
Rob Wagner's Script
San Diego Magazine
Saturday Night
Screen Album Magazine
Screen Guide
Screenland
Screenlife
Screenplay
Southwest Builder and Contractor
Stage
Time
Venice Vanguard
Weekly Variety
Westways

Academy of Motion Picture Arts and Sciences/Margaret Herrick Library, p. 171; American Stock, p. 70; AP/Wide World, pp. 56, 63, 65, 69, 112, 132, 188, 194, 211, 217 (top); Author's collection, pp. 8, 9, 11, 12, 13, 14, 15, 16, 17, 20, 21, 22, 24, 26 (bottom), 28 (bottom left), 29, 31, 34, 35 (bottom), 40 (bottom), 42, 46 (right), 48, 50–55, 72 (bottom), 75 (bottom), 79, 81 (bottom), 85–89, 91 (bottom), 92, 102 (left), 109 (left), 110, 111 (bottom), 115 (top), 117, 125, 126, 129, 134, 136 (bottom), 139, 140 (bottom), 141, 142, 144, 145 (top), 145 (bottom), 146 (bottom), 147, 152–57, 161, 162 (bottom), 163, 164 (bottom), 165, 168 (top), 170 (right), 174 (right), 175 (bottom), 176, 177, 178 (bottom), 180, 181 (bottom), 182, 186 (right), 189 (bottom), 190, 191, 192, 204–6, 208, 209 (top), 210, 212 (top), 216 (bottom), 217 (bottom); Roger Beerworth, p. 170 (left); Bison Archives/Mark Wanamaker, pp. 40 (top), 45, 46 (left), 58 (top), 59, 64, 68, 73, 81 (top), 82, 83 (top), 90, 96, 97, 100, 102 (right), 103–8, 115 (bottom), 116, 119 (bottom), 120, 124, 127, 128, 131, 133, 135, 137, 145 (middle), 146 (top), 164 (top), 185, 186 (left), 187, 209 (bottom); California Historical Society, pp. 44, 72 (top), 121, 140 (top); California Outdoors and In, pp. 95, 118; California Pictorial, p. 168 (bottom); Dan Coombs, p. 25 (top); Ralph Crane/Life Magazine/Time Inc., pp. 197, 198, 201–3; Culver City Historical Society, pp. 18 (bottom), 26 (top), 27, 28 (bottom right); Bruce Henstell, pp. 6, 18 (top), 41 (bottom), 71 (bottom), 76, 80 (bottom), 113, 169, 196; Joe Jasgur, pp. 173, 199, 212 (bottom), 213–15; Alan Magill, p. 109 (right); Dave Marshall, pp. 130, 179; Pictorial California, p. 119 (top); Pomona Library/Frasher Collection, pp. 74, 200; George Vernon Russell, p. 184; Security Pacific National Bank Photographic Collection/Los Angeles Public Library (SPNBPC/LAPL), pp. 25 (bottom), 28 (top), 66, 80 (top), 94, 160, 216 (top); Times Mirror Press/UCLA Special Collections, p. 10; Bruce Torrence, pp. 35 (top), 111 (top), 178 (top); UCLA/Daily News Collection, pp. 67, 166, 167, 181 (top), 189 (top), 195, 207; Variety Arts Archives, pp. 172, 174; Whittington Collection/California State University at Long Beach Special Collections (CSULB/SC), pp. 19, 30, 32, 33, 36, 37, 38, 39, 41 (top), 58 (bottom), 61, 62, 71 (top), 75 (top), 78, 84, 91 (top), 93, 98, 101, 114, 122, 123, 136 (top), 138, 143, 148–51, 162 (top); Jack Wilkes/Life Magazine/Time Inc., p. 193.

223

Boldface page numbers refer to photographs.